Mastering Baseball

Mastering Baseball

Dick Groch

Photography by Ralph Polovich

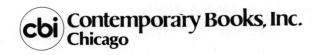 **cbi** **Contemporary Books, Inc.**
Chicago

Library of Congress Cataloging in Publication Data

Groch, Dick.
   Mastering baseball.

   Includes index.
   1. Baseball.   I. Title.
GV867.G763   796.357'2   77-91156
ISBN 0-8092-7816-2
ISBN 0-8092-7815-4 pbk.

Published by Contemporary Books, Inc.
180 North Michigan Avenue, Chicago, Illinois 60601
Manufactured in the United States of America
Library of Congress Catalog Card Number: 77-91156
International Standard Book Number: 0-8092-7816-2 (cloth)
                                     0-8092-7815-4 (paper)

Published simultaneously in Canada by
Beaverbooks
953 Dillingham Road
Pickering, Ontario L1W 1Z7
Canada

Contents

Preface

Mastering Baseball was written to improve the quality of America's number one pastime. It is intended to offer an in-depth study of how the game of baseball should be played. The material is presented in a manner that will allow players and coaches at all levels of competition to become better acquainted with the skills of an outstanding baseball player must have. From the Little League player to the college coach, from the professional baseball player to the summer league manager, from the budding high school star to the armchair devotee, *Mastering Baseball* offers something for all.

The fundamentals of position play are explained in detail and made clear by the use of exceptional photography. In conjunction with the "hows" of position play, there is a comprehensive chapter on baseball drills that can be used to assist you in the development of your skills.

Departing from the traditional inclusion of standard cut-offs and relays, the book includes a look at some of the special plays you can use to spice up your team's play. Additional chapters cover conditioning, helpful hints for young baseball players, and the responsibilities of being a Big League manager.

Whether you are interested in fundamentals, learning to play a new position, improving play at your present position, picking up a helpful coaching point, or broadening your knowledge and appreciation of the game, *Mastering Baseball* was written for you.

Mastering Baseball

FAST BALL—The four-seam grip is easier to control, and the ball will have a tendency to look smaller coming to home plate. When the proper spin is applied, the seams blend together, making the ball look smaller.

FAST BALL—Gripping the ball in this way will cause it to sink. The sinking action of the pitch will result in the batter hitting the ball on the ground.

CURVE BALL—The curve ball grip should be the same as the grip used for the fast ball.

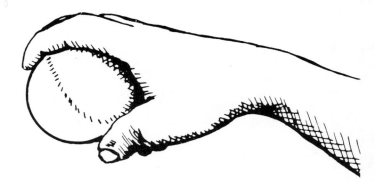

SLIDER—For the slider, the ball is held slightly off-center.

CHANGE-UP—The change-up is held deep in the pitching hand. The deeper it is held, the more difficult it becomes to throw with velocity.

KNUCKLEBALL—A very difficult pitch to learn to throw.

FORKBALL—The forkball is thrown by pitchers with large fingers. It is thrown as an off-speed pitch. When thrown properly, it will have a tendency to sink.

Forkball

The forkball is another method of throwing an off-speed pitch. The forkball, when properly thrown, has a reverse spin that causes the ball to sink. It is a difficult pitch for pitchers with small fingers.

WINDUP

There are three types of windups used by pitchers today: the full windup, the three-quarter windup, and the no windup.

The windup is nothing more than a technique used to get the body in motion preliminary to the delivery of the pitch to the plate. The no windup method was first used by pitchers who had control problems. The theory was that the less movement generated by the body, the less to coordinate, and the less to coordinate, the smaller the margin for pitching error.

Regardless of the method employed, the pitcher must keep his eyes on the target. The ball is well hidden in the pocket of his glove, and his foot is in contact with the rubber. As the pitcher begins his pivot, the toes are over the front edge of the rubber with the weight transferred to the bent back leg.

As his movement toward the plate begins, the pitcher still maintains a bent back leg for maximum body push. As he strides forward to deliver the pitch, the stride leg lands on the ball of the foot, about four inches to the left of a straight line from the toe of the right foot to home plate.

The pitcher then transfers his weight to the bent stride leg, continues the important follow through, and assumes a fielding position.

PITCHING FROM THE STRETCH

Working from the stretch position, the pitcher must not only contend with the batter but he must be responsible for holding the runner close to first base. Holding the runner close will give him a chance for a play at second base in case of a bunt. It also gives the catcher a chance to throw the runner out on a steal attempt and the outfielders an opportunity to prevent the runner from advancing to third base on a single.

The pitcher may use what is referred to as a short stretch, or he may employ a long stretch. Most pitchers learn both maneuvers.

The hands are always held at the waist, never above or below. The front foot is slightly open for a better view of the runner at first base. The right leg is flexed for maximum push-off from the rubber. The shoulders must not rotate away from the hitter, nor should the pitcher make an exaggerated leg kick in delivering the pitch to the plate. Such pitching mistakes give the runner at first a big jump toward second base on an attempted steal.

PICKOFF MOVES TO FIRST AND SECOND BASE

The right-handed pitcher makes his throw to first base by pivoting on his right foot and stepping toward first base with his left foot. He should be able to throw from three positions: with his hands held high, with hands halfway down, and from a set position.

To pick an opponent off of second base, the pitcher makes a jump shift toward the glove side. Remember, the actual throw to second base need not be made; it is not a balk. If you do not have a play at second base, don't throw the ball. Another method popular with some pitchers is to turn toward the throwing side for the throw to second base.

FOOT POSITION IN WINDUP— Right-handed pitchers will pitch from the right side of the rubber. The toes extend over the rubber to allow the foot to pivot properly. Once the pivot is completed, the pivot foot is flat against the rubber, ready for the push-off.

WINDUP—(Opposite page) In this sequence the pitcher is demonstrating the mechanics of the three-quarter windup. This is a study of intense concentration on the pitching target. (Mark Fidrych)

WINDUP—(Opposite page and this page) The no windup method allows the pitcher to be more compact in his delivery. Notice the weight being transferred to the back leg in preparation for a forceful delivery to the plate. (Pat Dobson)

WINDUP—(Opposite page and this page) The full windup brings the hands completely overhead. The ball must remain well hidden in the pitcher's glove. The leg kick is not exaggerated, but controlled. As the pitcher comes forward to deliver the pitch, the stride leg lands on the ball of the foot. The follow through is completed as the arm continues its smooth flow to the opposite side of the body. (Bill Lee)

FOOT POSITION IN THE STRETCH—When working from the stretch, the back foot must stay in contact with the rubber. The stride foot will be opened to help facilitate proper hip action. Opening the right foot also will put the pitcher in a position to get a better look at the runner at first base without opening his front shoulder.

PITCHING FROM THE STRETCH—(Left and opposite page) With hands held at waist level, the leg kick must be smooth and quick. This sequence illustrates how the eyes pick up the target after checking the runner at first base. Notice how the stride leg opens to allow for rotation of the back hip and transfer of weight to the stride foot. (Mark Fidrych)

COVERING FIRST BASE—On all balls hit to the right side, the pitcher must get over quickly to cover the base. (Chris Knapp and Jim Spencer)

COVERING FIRST BASE

On any ball hit to the right side, the pitcher must automatically break toward first base. Some teams make it mandatory for the catcher to shout to the pitcher as a reminder to cover first.

There are two recommended methods for handling this play. On the ball hit directly to the first baseman or to his left, the pitcher should move to a spot approximately 10 to 12 feet on the home plate side of first base and then run toward first parallel to the line. The pitcher gets to the line as quickly as he can; it's not until he starts to run parallel with the line that he slows down to get himself under control.

He will receive the ball about chest high, a good stride or two from the base. After he tags the inside of the bag, he immediately gets into position to make a play on any advancing runner.

On a ball hit far to the right of the first baseman, or on a ball that he fumbles, the pitcher should get to the bag by running directly from the pitching rubber to first base. The pitcher then takes the throw as a first baseman would, placing one foot on the second base side of the bag.

FIELDING THE BUNT

In all bunt situations the proper mental attitude of the pitcher is of vital importance. By mental attitude, we refer to the pitcher playing offensive baseball. He will not give into the bunting team and play defense. With all bunts, the pitcher is mentally and physically thinking about making the play at the advancing base until directed otherwise by his catcher. With a runner on first base, the pitcher will charge the ball with his body slightly opened toward second base. His weight is distributed toward the back foot, crotch down, right hand on top of the left, and head down.

With runners on first and second and the bunt in order, the pitcher must be prepared to cover the third base line.

The pitcher should position himself so that he will be able to rotate counterclockwise and throw to third base. Fielding and throwing should be all one motion, with the throw slightly sidearm.

DEFENDING AGAINST THE SQUEEZE

With a runner on third base, the pitcher must not rule out the possibility of the runner stealing home or the opponents executing the squeeze play. Working from the stretch often places the pitcher in an advantageous position to defend properly in these situations. However, with a runner in scoring position, the pitcher may feel that he can get a little bit extra by taking a windup.

Working with a runner at third base, there is a recommended procedure for a pitcher to follow. Get your sign from the catcher, look at the runner, look home, pick up your target, and pitch. It also helps to use a short, or three-quarter, windup. Some pitchers use no wind up in this situation.

COVERING HOME PLATE

On short passed balls or wild pitches, the pitcher may find it necessary to cover home and make a play on the runner attempting to score from third base. He should get to the plate as quickly as possible, drop his right foot toward the diamond to prevent injury, and make the tag with the ball well protected from the runner. Tag as quickly as possible and get the glove out of the way.

ESTABLISHING A PITCHING ROUTINE

The pitching routine used will depend on whether you are a starting pitcher, a starter who is used in relief, or primarily a relief pitcher.

A recommended routine for a starting pitcher who is a member of a four-man rotation is to pitch 10 to 15 minutes of batting practice the day after pitching, rest on the third day, and be prepared to start on the fourth day. Throwing batting practice is recommended for pitchers who need work on their control. It provides an opportunity to throw to a catcher and a batter.

An alternate to pitching batting practice is to throw 10 to 15 minutes on the sidelines. The pitcher should do his throwing under a coach's supervision. On the sidelines, the pitcher will work on his curve ball and his off-speed pitches, with emphasis on control.

A starting pitcher who is used in relief should avoid throwing batting practice, If you are asked to warm up but are not used in the game, the next day will be your day of rest prior to your next start. If it was not necessary for you to warm up and it is apparent that you will not be needed to relieve, you should get your 10 to 15 minutes of throwing near the end of the game.

As a starting pitcher, you should not be expected to pitch in relief the day after pitching a full game or the equivalent of a full game.

If you are used as a relief pitcher and are asked to warm up, be sure you loosen up the first time you get up to throw. Once you are adequately warmed up, you will not need to throw as much if you continue to throw for the next inning or two. If you get a hurried warm up call, you should be ready after throwing 15 to 20 pitches.

As a relief pitcher, you should be able to throw an inning or two for three days in a row. However, if you pitch for more than three innings in any game, your next day should be your rest day before you are asked to pitch again.

If your starting pitchers have had exceptional success and your services have not been required for three or four consecutive days, pitch 15 to 20 minutes of batting practice, then rest for a day before relieving.

FIELDING THE BUNT—(Opposite page and above) Communication is important on all bunt plays. Here the pitcher calls for the bunt. When fielding the bunt, the pitcher bends his knees, looks the ball into the glove, and uses his top hand as a guide. After fielding the bunt, he opens up his front hip, picks up the target, and prepares to throw the runner out at first base.

2

Behind the Mask— Catching with Skill

It is difficult to field a winning baseball team without a top-flight catcher. Second to pitching, strong catching will allow your team to experience a successful season. It has been said that catching is the shortest route to the major leagues. It is a difficult position to master and one that is physically demanding. As a catcher, you are more involved in the games you play than a player at any other position. You will be responsible for directing cut-offs, studying batters, and keeping your team mentally alert. The catcher is the "quarterback" of a baseball team, he serves as the "coach on the field," and he is your team leader.

To become a catcher, you need to work hard and sacrifice much. It is because of the physical and mental demands of this position that many young players avoid becoming catchers. If, however, you are willing to commit yourself to becoming an outstanding catcher, you will reap the satisfaction of knowing that you were intricately involved in the success of your team.

GIVING THE SIGNALS

Keep the signal well hidden from the opposing coaches. If your knees are pointing at the pitcher and toes are turned in, you should be able to keep the signals well hidden.

BASIC CATCHING POSITIONS

There are two suggested positions for the catcher to assume with no runner on base. Some organizations allow their catchers to get down on one knee. This provides the pitcher with a low target and the umpire with an opportunity to take a better look at the low pitch.

GIVING THE SIGNAL—When giving the signal, be sure to protect against the base coaches stealing your sign. (Ernie Whitt)

BASIC POSITION—With no one on base, the catcher will get as low as possible and provide the pitcher with a suitable target. The throwing hand should be out of the way to protect against being hit by a foul ball.

RUNNER ON FIRST BASE—When a runner occupies first base, the catcher must come up into the throwing position. The right foot is slightly open, and the throwing hand is positioned behind the glove.

Another position is the squatting stance, with the buttocks below the line of the knees. In either position, the catcher must take extra care to protect his throwing hand. It is recommended that he receive the pitch with the glove hand only, keeping the throwing hand out of the way.

With a runner on base, the catcher must get the weight of the buttocks up to knee level. This position improves his mobility. The right foot is slightly open and is used as a platform to push off when fielding a bunt or throwing to the bases. He now becomes a two-handed catcher. The throwing hand is placed alongside of the glove, ready to grasp the ball, after catching it, for a quick throw to retire an advancing runner.

RECEIVING THE PITCH

The term used to describe catching a baseball is "patterning the pitch." This does not mean that you "pull" the ball into the strike zone; you simply catch a strike in the strike zone.

The pitch below the knees is caught and patterned upward. The high pitch is patterned downward. The catcher receives the outside pitch backhand and slightly rotates the elbow to keep the ball in the strike zone. The inside pitch is patterned with an inward position of the glove.

Many young players ask about catching the curve ball. If you have difficulty catching the curve in the strike zone, you may find it helpful to reach out for the low curve. The high curve should be caught close to the body.

THROWING TO THE BASES

Always use the four-seam grip when throwing to the bases; gripping the ball in this manner prevents the ball from dipping, tailing, or sinking.

There is no single right way to throw to second base; the catcher should use the method that works best for him. His objective, of course, is to get the ball to second base ahead of the runner and with accuracy and velocity.

The best method calls for the catcher to receive the ball and, in one smooth, uninterrupted motion, get it into position to throw. He will throw from the ear, and always overhand.

The throw to second base should be made as quickly as possible. There is no need for unnecessary footwork. The catcher should push directly off his right foot and throw.

On occasion, the catcher will find it necessary to throw to third base. The mechanics of making this throw are much the same as making the throw to second base, except on pitches that are inside to right-handed batters. In these situations, the catcher may want to throw from behind the batter without altering his basic footwork, or he may choose to drop back one step before throwing.

On the ball down the middle of the plate or to the outside corner, the catcher needs to raise the elbow of his glove hand. The elbow should be driven toward the batter's chest to be sure the batter does not serve as an obstruction to the throw to third.

FIELDING THE BUNT

When the ball is bunted out in front of the plate, the catcher must "loop" the ball slightly to get his body in the proper position to throw to first base. The glove hand is used to help guide the ball into the throwing hand.

On the bunt down the first-base line, the catcher will run directly toward the ball. He guides the ball into the glove, drops to the inside of the diamond with his rear leg, and throws overhand to first base. The drop-step and the overhand throw will help prevent hitting the runner going to first base.

The most difficult of the three bunts for the catcher to handle, because of the time it takes to get his body into throwing position, is the bunt down the third-base line. The catcher should run directly toward the ball,

HIGH PITCH—Catch the high pitch by tipping the glove slightly forward. (John Wockenfuss)

LOW PITCH—On low pitches uses an underhand motion. This will assist you in keeping the ball in the strike zone.

INSIDE PITCH—The inside pitch should be caught with the glove turned in toward the plate.

OUTSIDE PITCH—After catching a pitch on the outside corner of the plate, rotate the elbow upward. The action of rotating the elbow will guide the pitch into the strike zone.

GRIP FOR THROWING—Always use the four-seam grip, which will put a better "carry" on the ball. After securing the proper grip, the ball should be brought to the ear quickly and thrown overhand.

THROWING TO SECOND BASE—As the ball is caught, the weight is rapidly shifted to the right foot. The catcher will point the front shoulder in the direction of his throw, step toward his target with his left foot, and throw.

THROWING TO SECOND BASE (SIDE VIEW)—A side view provides a study of the catcher's footwork. Take notice of how the ball is caught with two hands. It takes hours of practice to get the ball quickly out of the glove and into throwing position.

BUNT DOWN FIRST BASE LINE—On a bunt down the first base line, the catcher will guide the ball into his throwing hand with his glove. He then drops the back foot, picks up his target, and throws to first base.

BUNT DOWN THIRD BASE LINE—The catcher runs directly at the ball, fielding it off the instep of his right foot. It is important to pick up your target quickly and step in the direction of your throw.

GETTING RID OF THE MASK—Grab the mask and hold it securely. Once you locate the ball, you may discard the mask and make the catch.

overstepping with his right foot, guide the ball with his glove, pivot, and throw to first base. The throw will be overhand, with the lead foot (the left foot) stepping directly toward first base.

MAKING THE HOME-TO-FIRST DOUBLE PLAY

To execute this play, the catcher must quickly remove his mask and place his right foot on home plate, ready to make the force out on the runner coming from third. He will step toward the throw only after it has been made by the infielder and he can see that it is a good one. Stepping forward too early places him in a poor position to handle a bad throw. After receiving the throw, he will step quickly to the inside of the diamond with the right foot and throw to first base. Stepping into the diamond will get him out of the way of the runner sliding into home, trying to break up the double play.

CATCHING POP-UPS

Most pop-ups are misplayed by catchers who fail to get into proper position to make the catch. Remember, as a ball travels upward, it travels away from home plate; as the ball starts its descent, it moves back toward the plate. The catcher must quickly remove his mask, holding on to it until he

locates the ball. After locating the ball, he will discard the mask in a direction opposite that in which he is running. The catch will be made above his eyes, using both hands. If he has trouble with the sun, he will use either his glove or his throwing hand to shield his eyes.

HANDLING BAD PITCHES

Defensively, the ball in the dirt ranks as the catcher's most difficult play. On the ball that hits directly in front of him, the catcher must learn to drop to both knees, roll his chest forward, and keep his shoulders square. He must be sure to tuck his chin into his chest to prevent injury to the throat. The ball should be cushioned by the chest.

On bad pitches to his left or right, the catcher must remember the importance of getting his body in front of the ball. This

CATCHING POP FLYS—Catch all pop flies above eye level, using two hands. If you are having problems with the sun, learn to use your glove to shade your eyes.

BALL IN THE DIRT—On the ball in the dirt, notice how the catcher rolls his shoulders forward and gets his chin on his chest. The throwing hand is protected by tucking the thumb into the hand.

will allow him to block with his chest and keep the ball in front of him. With the ball in front, the catcher can recover it quickly and prevent the advance of a base runner.

TAG PLAY AT HOME PLATE

One of the most exciting plays in baseball is the tag play at home plate. This play happens so quickly that well-taught fundamentals are often disregarded.

The catcher should position himself by placing his left foot in front of and slightly to the left of home plate. He must remember that it is illegal for him to block home plate unless he has possession of the ball.

The toes of the left foot should point toward third base. With the foot in this position, the knee will be free to bend if contact is made with an incoming runner. Turning the left foot so that it is facing the center of the diamond makes the catcher a prime candidate for either a knee or ankle injury.

There are only three ways a runner will come into home plate. He will slide straight in, hook slide, or try to run through the catcher. If he hook slides, he does you a favor because he is easy to tag while avoiding contact. Every time contact is avoided, the possibility of incurring a serious injury is reduced.

All young catchers must remember to catch the ball before attempting to make a tag. Don't leave the plate to catch the ball and come back to make the tag. The ball will get to you; make the play when the throw arrives.

Always make the tag with two hands. Protect the ball by forcing the runner to slide into the back of the glove. The ball should be held in the ungloved hand. Keep the hand holding the ball several inches behind the glove, allowing the runner to slide into the glove. This forces the glove into contact with the ball. It is dangerous to thrust the throwing hand entirely into the glove; this could result in a wrist injury.

SHIFTING RIGHT—This catcher demonstrates the footwork required in making the shift.

SHIFTING LEFT—Pay special attention to how hard the catcher works to angle his shoulders in toward the center of the field.

On occasion, the catcher will find it necessary to use a sweep tag. This type of tag may be used when the runner has every intention of knocking the catcher down at the plate. Instead of taking him head on, use the sweep tag. This maneuver is especially useful on throws up the third base line. It is important to execute the play by tagging the oncoming runner with two hands.

PASSED BALL

Two methods are taught to handle the passed ball or the wild pitch in situations where the ball gets by the catcher and the runner on third base attempts to score. One method is to get to the ball as soon as possible, overstep, and throw to the man covering home plate from the position used to field the ball. The other method requires the catcher to drop to one knee. Keeping the ball on the inside of the right foot, he delivers the throw to the pitcher, who is covering home plate.

TAG PLAY AT THE PLATE—Protect the ball by holding it in your entire hand, and cover your bare hand with your catcher's glove.

PASSED BALL—Get to the ball as quickly as possible and throw from the position in which you field the ball.

3
Defending First Base

The qualifications for playing first base are not as demanding as they are for other infielders. A study of present day Major League first basemen provides us with an image of the big, strong power hitter, the man in the lineup who will deliver the much needed extra base hit and will be among the team leaders in runs batted in. Prime examples of modern first basemen are: John Mayberry, Tony Perez, Willie McCovey, Jason Thompson, George Scott, Dick Allen, and Lee May.

Most players adapt quickly to playing first base. Many of the great players of our time prolonged their careers by making the transition from their original position. Former New York Yankee and Hall of Famer, Mickey Mantle, made the successful move to first base.

It is not necessary for a first baseman to demonstrate great speed or an outstanding throwing arm. It is required, however, that the first basemen provide the infielders with an excellent target. He also must demonstrate mobility to handle all types of errant throws and enough arm strength to throw out a runner advancing from second to third or a runner tagging at third and attempting to score on a foul fly down the right-field line.

In all fairness to a position subject to much abuse, it should be pointed out that first base has been occupied by some of the slickest fielders in baseball history. Wes Parker, Gil Hodges, and George Scott all demonstrated prowess with the glove.

QUALIFICATIONS

Ideally, your first baseman should be tall, quick, and a fine fielder of ground balls. It

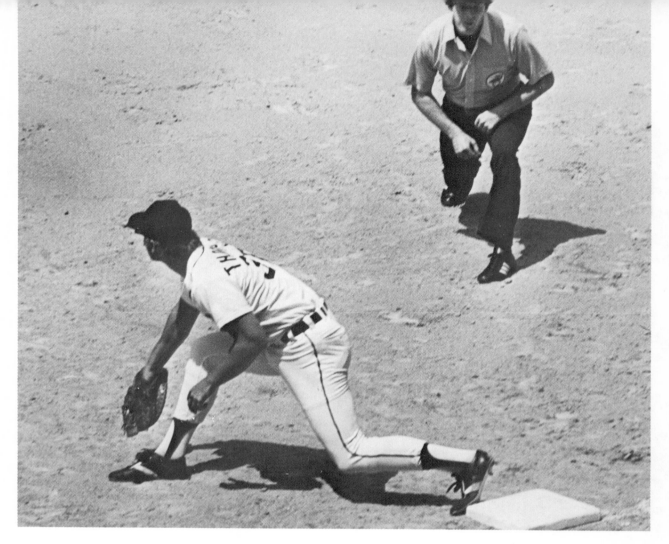

TAKING THE THROW—Always step in the direction of the throw. Be careful not to pull your foot off of the base. Umpires will watch you closely. (Jason Thompson)

is also to his advantage to be left-handed. Since the majority of his throws are to his right, he will be able to make these plays more quickly than the right-handed first baseman. The right-handed first baseman must shift his body prior to throwing to second or third. The left-handed first baseman also has an advantage in fielding ground balls, since he must move to his right and cover as much ground as possible. He increases the range of the entire right side of the infield. The farther a first baseman can range to his right, the farther the second baseman can play toward second base. Moving the second baseman toward his base reduces the number of base hits lost up the middle.

RECEIVING THROWS

There are two basic methods of taking throws at first base. The simplest is referred to as the "shift" method. The other is the "cross-over" method, generally reserved for the more agile player. The "shift" method is described below.

On all ground balls, the first baseman must get to his base as quickly as possible and face the throw with legs bent for mobility and arms hanging loosely. The heels of both feet are on the bag.

From this stance, the first baseman can shift his body to any position to catch a throw that is slightly off-line. A first baseman must remember that in the event of a wild throw, it is much more to his advan-

COMING OFF THE BASE—At times it will be necessary to leave the base and take a bad throw. Do not attempt to locate the base; attempt to tag the runner.

tage to leave the bag and catch the ball than to let the ball get by him, allowing the runner to go to second base. He must get off the bag, catch the ball, and attempt to tag the runner on his way by.

The most difficult ball for the first baseman to handle is one thrown into the dirt. Here, the soft-handed first baseman becomes an asset. He must not slap at the ball. His glove should first be placed in the dirt, then used to guide the ball to his body. Learning to keep his head down on this play will make it easier to execute.

Regardless of the type of throw, good or bad, the first baseman is responsible for receiving it. He must not commit himself until the ball has been thrown by the in-fielder. He should stride in the direction of the throw, with his stride foot hitting the ground as the ball hits his glove.

PLAYING POSITION BASEBALL

One of the most difficult aspects of playing first base is knowing where to play according to the game situation. The young player just beginning his career as a first baseman may find it necessary to rely on his manager for proper positioning.

Normally, with no one out, the first baseman will play 12 to 15 feet behind the bag. This basic position may be altered according to the hitter's strength. With a right-handed pull hitter, the first baseman will move toward second base. When the batter

HOLDING THE RUNNER AT FIRST BASE—When holding the runner at first base, provide the pitcher with an adequate target.

is a left-handed pull hitter, the first baseman will play deeper and closer to the line to protect against the extra base hit. This is especially true in the late innings with the defense ahead.

With a runner on first base, the first baseman will find it necessary to alter his basic fielding position. Now, he must hold the runner on base. He will assume a position on the inside corner of the bag and provide the pitcher with a suitable target, should the pitcher throw to first in an attempt to pick the runner off or to hold him close to the bag. If the pitcher does throw over, the first baseman must catch the ball and immediately apply the tag to the inside of first base. He must not wildly attempt to tag the runner; remember, the runner must return to the bag to be safe. The first baseman must be careful not to get "picked-off," that is, he must be absolutely certain that the pitcher will deliver the pitch to the plate before he shuffles into fielding position.

At times it will be necessary for the first baseman to play behind the runner at first base. When he does, it will be his responsibility to notify the pitcher of his position change. This will prevent the pitcher from throwing to first base when the first baseman is not in position. When the pitcher knows that the first baseman is playing behind the runner, a balk also will be avoided.

The first baseman may be directed to play behind a slow runner at first. With a good runner at first, he may play behind the runner when his team is ahead in the score. This does not mean the first baseman allows the runner unusual liberties at first base. He will still remain in a challenging position should the pitcher or catcher decide, by a prearranged signal, to attempt a pickoff play.

On occasion, the manager will position the first baseman as deep as possible with a runner on first base. This would be the case

BREAKING FROM FIRST BASE—Following the pitcher's delivery to the plate, the first baseman will shuffle off into his basic fielding position.

in situations involving a left-handed pull-hitter, two outs, a 3–2 count on the batter, and the defense holding at least a two-run lead.

With runners on first and second and the bunt not in order, the first baseman should play behind the runner at first base. He must remain in a challenging position to the runner. Keeping the runner close at first retains the possibility of a double play and prevents the runner from scoring from first on a long double.

DEFENDING AGAINST THE BUNT

One of the more difficult situations for a first baseman to handle is the bunt play. He must defend against the bunt when there is a runner on first or runners on first and second.

With a runner on first, the first baseman will play a step or two off first base in the direction of home plate. The first baseman will charge toward home when the pitcher delivers his pitch to the batter. If the ball is bunted, the catcher will direct the play. He will instruct the fielders as to where the play will be made, first or second base, and who will field the bunt, the pitcher or the first baseman.

We readily can see why a left-handed first baseman is preferred. The "lefty" is in position to field the bunt quickly with both hands and make a fast throw to either second or third. Note, we said *field the ball with both hands*. There will be the isolated situation where the first baseman will be required to pick up the ball with his bare hand and make the play on the advancing runner; this is not without risk.

If the bunted ball should be bobbled, do not give up on the play. Do not attempt to pick up the ball with your glove; it may stick in the webbing or be bobbled a second time. Pick up the misplayed ball with the bare hand and make the play on the batter.

THE DOUBLE PLAY

Nothing can be more important to the first baseman than turning the 3–6–3 double play. The double play has saved many ball games by getting pitchers out of deep trouble. Again the value of the left-handed first baseman becomes apparent. After fielding the double play ball, the left-handed first baseman can throw to second base from the position in which he fields the ball or after taking a slight shuffle step toward second. If the first baseman fields the ball behind first base, the throw to the shortstop covering second base must be to the center field side of second.

When the ball is fielded in front of first base, the throw will be made to the infield side of second base. In either case, the first baseman must be careful not to hit the advancing runner with his throw. The right-handed first baseman must "jump shift" his body to get into proper position to make a good throw.

After throwing to second, the first baseman will turn toward his glove side in returning to first base for the shortstop's throw. Under no circumstances should the first baseman "back pedal" to return to first base. Back pedaling makes it easy for him to get his feet tangled, disrupts his balance, and puts him in a disadvantageous position to handle a poor throw.

On a ball hit near the bag, the first baseman may tag the bag before throwing to second base to complete the double play. However, tagging first base eliminates the force play at second base and the first baseman must remind the shortstop to tag the advancing runner.

PITCHER COVERING FIRST BASE

During every spring training, Major League teams require pitchers to spend hours practicing covering first base on balls hit to the right side. This drill serves as a 'constant reminder for the pitcher to break immediately toward first on balls that will be fielded by either the first or second baseman.

The pitcher will break quickly to a point

LEFT-HANDED ADVANTAGE—Being left-handed allows the first baseman to throw quickly to second base after fielding a ground ball.

approximately 10 or 12 feet from the bag, then run parallel with the line toward the bag. The first baseman will provide the pitcher with a firm, underhand toss at chest level. On occasion, an overhand throw may be necessary. This usually occurs when the first baseman ranges to his right and is too far away from his pitcher to make an effective underhand toss. The overhand toss should be firm, but it should not be thrown with such velocity that the pitcher has difficulty making the catch. Remember, the pitcher must catch the throw on the run and tag first base for the out, a more difficult task than it looks.

VERBAL COMMUNICATION

The first baseman will need hours of practice on ground balls hit to his right. He should know the instant the ball is hit whether it will be fielded by the second baseman or whether he can successfully complete the play. The second baseman will assist by quickly calling off the first baseman as soon as he is certain that he will be able to field the ball.

The other defensive situation requiring verbal communication is when the ball is hit slowly between the pitcher's mound and the first base bag. Most Big League first basemen consider this play the most difficult one of all. If the ball is fielded by the pitcher, the first baseman will find it necessary to return quickly to first base. If the first baseman is forced to field the ball, then he must feed the pitcher, who is approaching first base with his back partially turned to his first baseman. The pitcher should call off the first baseman on all balls he can handle by saying, "I've got it." On balls that he wants his first baseman to field, he should call, "Take it."

On all unassisted putouts, the first baseman will both call off and wave off the pitcher. This will avoid any collision at first base between pitcher and first baseman.

4
Guardian
of the Keystone—
the Second Baseman

The second baseman comprises half of the heart of the infield. He will need to start quickly, have good range, sure hands, coordination, and good reflexes.

Arm strength for the second baseman is not as crucial as it would be for the shortstop or the third baseman. The second baseman's arm is tested on balls hit behind second base that require him to backhand the ball and throw to first base. Similar to this is the play that forces the second baseman to range far to his left to field the ball and then throw to the shortstop covering second base for the force out. A good throwing arm may also prove beneficial when the second baseman is serving as a relay man on a play at the plate or when he catches a pop fly down the right field line and attempts to throw out the runner tagging at third base. On these plays a second baseman with a strong throwing arm is desirable.

More important than a strong throwing arm is the ability of the second baseman to throw from various arm positions, i.e., over the top, sidearm, three-quarter, and underhand. These are the throws required by a second baseman, and if you intend to play that position, you should work on them in practice sessions. However, before working on these throws, warm up properly and include three or four off-balance throws in your warm up routine. If you want to strengthen your arm as well as stretch it out, practice long throws. Remember, a young player can compensate for a weak arm with quickness and fundamental execution.

The second baseman must be a good fielder of ground balls. A good infielder must charge every ground ball in order to gauge its bounce, or hop. If he fails to charge right away, he loses his perception of how the ball is bouncing. The most difficult chance for the infielder is the ball hit straight at him because he has a tendency to wait for the ball. Usually, an infielder misses a ball when he gets caught flat-footed. If he stands in one place and the ball takes any kind of unexpected hop, he is in trouble. Go toward the ball, especially if it is hit right at you.

One of the more common questions asked about fielding ground balls concerns the ball hit up the middle: who has priority, the shortstop or the second baseman? Usually, the shortstop should be given the opportunity to make this play since his body momentum is carrying him toward first base.

CATCHING FLY BALLS

Pop-ups can present the infielder with some difficulty. When attempting to catch a pop-up, try to keep the ball on the glove side. It will be easier to catch the pop-up on the forehand rather than the backhand side.

Avoid back pedaling when going back for pop flies; it results in tangled feet and misplayed balls. We recommend that the fielder turn sideways on all fly balls.

Communication on fly balls is very important and will prevent serious injury to the players. Prior to the season, the manager should determine who is responsible for catching fly balls in certain areas of the field and what type of communication system will be used. Normally, the second baseman will take priority over the first baseman on any ball hit down the right field line. The first baseman will attempt to make every catch unless he hears the second baseman call, "I have it."

On fly balls hit between the second baseman and the outfielders, the second baseman will attempt to make all catches unless he is called off by the outfielders. As soon as the outfielder calls for the ball, the second baseman should immediately yield the right of way.

Most players who have problems with pop-ups run flat-footed rather than on the balls of their feet. Running flat-footed causes the ball to appear to be jumping—an optical illusion. If the player feels that he is running on the balls of his feet but the ball still is jumping, he should glance away from the ball for a moment. He should continue to run in the direction he thinks the ball is falling and quickly pick up the ball again. This may be contrary to the old adage "never take your eyes off of the ball," but in this case it is fundamentally sound.

MAKING THE DOUBLE PLAY

There are several ways the second baseman can make the double-play pivot. The type of pivot selected depends on the type of throw he receives. It also depends on the physical assets of the person making the play. Every second baseman should "turn" the double play in the manner best suited to his physical abilities.

Initial positioning is very important to the success of a double play. With a runner at first base and the double play in order, the second baseman will assume double-play depth; this requires him to move three to five steps into the diamond and a step or two closer to the bag. When the batter grounds to the left side of the infield, the second baseman gets to his bag as quickly as he can, with his body under control. Being under control allows him to handle a bad throw and assures him of getting the lead runner.

After receiving the throw from the shortstop or third baseman, the second baseman may use the pivot most appropriate to complete the play. One method involves straddling the bag, touching the bag with the left foot, and throwing directly down the line to the first baseman. As Duane Kuiper (Cleveland Indians) explains, "I have to straddle the bag and come down the line with my throw because I don't have a strong throwing arm; this play is especially tough for me with a fast runner like Ron LeFlore (Detroit

Tigers) bearing down on me. You have to tell yourself to stay in on the play; if he knocks you down, it's part of the game."

A second popular pivot requires the second baseman to touch the bag with his left foot, push back away from the bag, plant his right foot, and throw. This method is advantageous when the runner from first base is advancing to second on the hit and run. It will help the second baseman get out of the way of a sliding runner and avoid contact.

Another method of completing the double play calls for the second baseman to cross the bag and throw to first. The second baseman steps on the base with his left foot and into the infield with his right foot. He pushes off with his right foot and steps toward first base to throw. He must employ a strong overhand throw to complete the double play on a rapidly advancing runner. This method of making the pivot can be used when the throw from the shortstop is late or when attempting the third-to-second-to-first double play.

Popular with some middlemen is the "drag and throw" technique. This usually requires a hard-hit ball to the shortstop or to the third baseman's left. Normally, the play is executed so quickly that the runner advancing to second does not constitute a threat to the safety of the second baseman. The second baseman receives the throw up the first base line or from the first base side of second. As the second baseman receives the throw, he drags his right foot across the bag and continues his movement to the infield side of the bag, stepping and throwing to first base.

MAKING THE THROWS

After fielding a ball hit directly at him, the second baseman will pivot in his tracks and make a chest-high throw to the shortstop covering second. On a ball hit to the second baseman's right, the second baseman will use an underhand toss. He will get the glove out of the way, show the shortstop the ball, and give him a firm, chest-high throw. It is important to step in the direction of your throw and to continue walking in its direction. This will result in a firm toss rather than one that hangs in the air.

When the ball is hit to the left of the second baseman, he must get in front of the ball and jump-step so that his body faces the direction of the throw. If the toe of the left foot is pointing in the direction of the throw, it will keep him from throwing against a locked hip. The throw should be sidearm or three-quarter.

On a ball hit deep to his left it will be necessary for the second baseman to field the ball and turn counterclockwise to make a firm, overhand throw to the shortstop. For a throw of this nature to have adequate velocity and accuracy, it must be made with balance and control.

The backhand flip is used when fielding the ball 15 to 18 feet away from the bag. A coach should not teach the player to flip the ball back to the shortstop while his momentum is carrying him toward the diamond. This is a difficult play and often results in a bad throw.

TAGGING THE RUNNER

When receiving a throw for purposes of making a tag, receive the throw with the knee bent. This will provide greater mobility should the ball skip or take a bad bounce.

When the throw is received, apply the tag with the ball in the lower part of the glove's webbing. Keep the back part of the glove toward the runner, make the tag quickly, and get the glove out of the way. This will prevent the sliding runner from kicking the ball out of the glove.

RUNDOWNS

There are some general rules applicable to all rundown situations. Always get the runner with no more than two throws. Run at him at full speed and employ the halfway rule. For example, when the second baseman has a runner trapped between second

DOUBLE PLAY PUSH BACK—After touching the base with the left foot, the second baseman will push back from the base and throw directly down the line to the first base. (Steve Dillard)

DOUBLE PLAY CROSSOVER—Following the drag of the right toe over the corner of the base, the weight must be transferred to the back foot. Getting the weight on the back foot prior to throwing allows you to get a little extra on your throw. The drag method also is used to get the force-out at second.

DOUBLE PLAY DRAG AND THROW—It is important that the second baseman receives the throw on the first base side of second base. Observe the way the second baseman hops on his left foot to avoid direct contact with the oncoming runner.

"PIVOT IN TRACKS"—
This ball has been hit
directly at the second
baseman. He pivots
without moving his feet
and gives the shortstop,
covering second, an
overhand throw. (Denny
Doyle)

THROW TO SECOND
BASE WHILE MOVING
LEFT—The second
baseman has moved to
his left to field a ground
ball. He shifts his body
toward second base,
drops to one knee, and
throws.

THROW TO SECOND BASE FROM DEEP TO HIS LEFT—(This page and opposite, top) Much more spectacular but not as effective is when the second baseman goes far to his left, leaps into the air, and throws to second base. It is difficult to make this throw with any velocity. The result is usually a force-out, with no chance of retiring the runner advancing to first base.

THROW TO SECOND BASE USING THE BACKHAND FLIP—It is important for the momentum of the body to be going in the direction of the throw. The backhand flip is a difficult technique to master.

RUNDOWN—A player in a rundown always seems to draw a crowd. Observe how the player on the right has "shortened up" to reduce the distance between himself, the runner, and the man with the ball.

and third, he should throw the ball to the third baseman when the runner is more than halfway to third base. The third baseman can then run the runner back to second, the base from which he started.

In the rundown the man with the ball will hold it in a three-quarter snap position. In this way the man catching can see the angle from which the ball will be thrown.

The man catching the ball should shade the bag to the throwing side of the man with the ball. This means that the third baseman would shade third base slightly to his left in taking a throw from the second baseman. This will reduce the possibility of the runner being hit with the ball.

A good fake works only when the runner is close enough to tag. However, never use more than one fake in a rundown. Faking takes too much time, and the only person "faked out" may be the third baseman.

After one fake, either make the tag or give the ball to the third baseman.

In certain situations, it is advisable for other infielders to leave their positions to help complete a rundown and make a tag. This is especially true with more than one runner on base. After the second baseman has completed his throw to the third baseman, the third baseman will run the runner back to second base, now being covered by the shortstop. When the runner is 18 to 20 feet away from second base, the shortstop will move toward the ball and yell, "Now," meaning that the ball should be thrown by the third baseman.

This procedure shortens the distance between the two infielders. It allows for a quicker tag and prevents the advance of other base runners. Tag with both hands, with the ball held by the throwing hand and in the glove for protection.

A TOUGH PLAY FOR A SECOND BASEMAN

As a coach with the Boston Red Sox, Johnny Pesky discussed the most difficult play at second base. "The slow roller, the ball you have to charge and throw across your body at a forty-five degree angle. That's got to be his toughest play." In making this play, the second baseman must . . . "aim his throw at the first baseman's right arm; this throw is made with the second baseman moving away from the direction in which he is throwing. As a result, the throw will be coming back or tailing away from the first baseman."

Another play Pesky refers to is the ball hit up the middle: "This can be a very difficult play for the second baseman, depending on how hard the ball is hit. Sometimes he has to come in and try to backhand the ball and flip it to first. If the ball is hit sharply, he can backhand the ball, brace himself, and take a little "crow hop" before he throws to first base. This will help him get something on the ball. This is what we try to teach our infielders in our minor-league system. We don't like anyone to throw the ball flat-footed because it's too easy to throw the ball away. If you make that nice, firm throw, nine times out of ten the runner will be out."

5
Defending the Hot Corner

When we mention the "hot corner," we immediately think of the man who made third base a household term, Brooks Robinson. Brooks made the most difficult plays at third base with such ease and perfection that the most acute baseball observers have classified him as incomparable.

Robinson's ability to go behind the bag and throw out a speedy runner at first base, his exceptional agility in charging a slowly hit ball and throwing accurately to first, and his fluid movement as he ranged far to his left to rob another frustrated hitter of a base hit, kept baseball fans constantly in awe.

It is beyond imagination that anyone in present-day baseball, or, for that matter, in baseball's future days, will play third base as flawlessly as the magician from Baltimore.

Golden Glove awards for outstanding defensive performance for a third baseman

went to Brooks Robinson as automatically as he knocked down hard-hit balls with his chest and threw runners out at first base. His selection year after year to the American League All-Star Team became as certain as his fielding a bunt with his bare hand and making an impossible throw to nip the runner at first base.

His performance against the Cincinnati Reds in the 1970 World Series will serve as the greatest one-man clinic on third base ever recorded in the annals of baseball history. I have been afforded many thrills in the game of baseball but none as memorable as having had the opportunity to watch Brooks Robinson play the "hot corner."

Playing third base does not require the foot speed needed to play second base or shortstop. A third baseman must have a strong, accurate arm, sure hands, and quick

FIELDING IN NORMAL POSITION—(This page and opposite) Backhanding the ball from his normal defensive position, the third baseman will throw straight overhand to retire a speedy runner advancing to first base. (Butch Hobson)

reactions. He will be required to block hard-hit balls with his chest, field slow-rolling bunts, and make long, accurate throws. A third baseman must possess quick reactions so that he will be able to field hard-hit balls without thinking.

He must be alert to the possibility of push bunts and drag bunts and react quickly to any change of hand position by the batter on the handle of the bat.

PROPER POSITIONING

Much of the success in playing any position revolves around knowing where to play in given situations and how to play the hitter.

With no one on base, the third baseman's normal fielding position is about 6 feet back of third base and about 10 feet inside the line.

With a right-handed pull-hitter at bat, he will play deeper and closer to the line to protect against the ball getting between him and the line for an extra-base hit. This is especially important with his team ahead in the game by one or two runs in the late innings.

The third baseman will play two or three steps in front of the base when there is a runner on first base and the bunt is in order or when the batter is a threat to bunt or is a fast runner.

With runners on first and second and the bunt in order, the third baseman will need to play two or three steps in front of the bag. He will have three major responsibilities in this situation. First, if the batter squares around as if to bunt but takes the pitch, the third baseman first charges toward the plate. When it becomes apparent that the batter will not bunt, he must quickly return to third base to defend against the possible steal. Second, if the ball is bunted to either the first baseman or straight back to the pitcher, he will find it

PROTECTING THE LINE—(This page and opposite) Play well behind third base to protect the line against an extra-base hit. The third baseman will get in front of the ball and make a strong, accurate throw to first base. (Eric Soderholm)

necessary to return quickly to third base and be prepared to receive a throw. Finally, his most difficult decision is whether or not to field a ball bunted between himself and the pitcher. This will involve hours of practice and communication between the pitcher and the third baseman.

A suggested method of handling this play is for the pitcher to field every ball bunted toward third base unless called off the play by the third baseman. Once the third baseman calls for the ball, it becomes his responsibility to field it and throw to the base directed by the catcher. This usually will mean a throw to first base, but occasionally the play will be made on the runner attempting to advance from first to second.

DOUBLE PLAY

There are two ways the third baseman may be involved in making the double play. Most often, the third baseman is involved in the "around-the-horn" double play—third-to-second-to-first. On this play we advise the third baseman to throw three-quarter or sidearm to the second baseman. This type of throw, slightly to the first base side of second and chest high, usually results in a quick double play.

On occasion, the third baseman will field a double play ball hit to his right and only three to four steps from the bag. To force a runner coming down from second, he should tag the bag with his right foot, using the bag to push-off, and throw overhand to first base.

MAKING A TOUGH PLAY

Butch Hobson, the exciting third baseman for the Boston Red Sox, shares with us his views on what he considers his toughest play.

"The slow chopper, not really a bunt, but

DOUBLE PLAY—When the third baseman fields a double play ball near the base, he will step on third and throw to first base. The third baseman can increase the velocity of his throw by using the bag to push off. (Buddy Bell)

the one that is hit and you have to make the decision to charge it or sit back on it. The ball isn't hit hard; its just got overspin on it. If you sit back on it and it hits close enough to you, you can let it hit you . . . in the chest and keep it in front. Or you can charge it, and if you get it as it's coming up, you can handle it with ease.

"Of course, the bunts are tough plays, but you don't get that many of them. The pitchers will try to get what they can. But if I am there, I will call him off. If it's a real good bunt, then I am going to make the play to first base . . . it's easier for me to make the play because the throw is in front of me. Of course, with a good fielding pitcher like Bill Lee, who gets off of the mound well, I will be able to relax a little more. With the way he gets to the ball, we also have the possibility of getting the runner at third base.

"Another play that can cause some problems is the double play situation where a left-handed batter is up. You are playing him to pull the ball to right, and he hits the ball to you at third base. We had a play like that in New York, runners on first and second, and Reggie Jackson up. He hit the ball to me, but I had to hold up because Denny Doyle was playing so far over. I had to wait for him to cover second base to be sure of getting at least the one out."

6
The Making of a Shortstop

The requirements for being a top-notch shortstop are considerably different than for any other position. The prime requirements are speed, a strong throwing arm, and a pair of good hands.

Let us take a moment to consider each characteristic. Note, we said speed; we did not say quickness. Quickness is necessary for catchers, third basemen, and first basemen. The shortstop needs to cover a considerable amount of ground, ranging from deep in the hole to behind the base at second. Getting to the ball requires *speed*. This point is exemplified by the large number of Major League shortstops that are generally among their team leaders in stolen bases. In this category would be such outstanding players as Larry Bowa, Fred Patek, Maury Wills, and Bert Campaneris. An interesting observation on the size of these players indicates that all are small in stature. Size is not a prerequisite to success at shortstop.

The second basic requirement of the shortstop is a strong throwing arm. Going in the hole, backhanding the ball, and throwing out a fast runner requires an outstanding arm. Another play on which the shortstop is required to exhibit a strong and accurate arm is the relay throw from the outfielder to the plate when attempting to cut down a runner trying to score from first base on a two-base hit. Without a strong accurate arm, the shortstop will have limited success.

The third basic necessity is a pair of quick hands. This is evident in making the double play, whatever the involvement of the shortstop. Whether getting the ball to the second baseman or making the pivot at the base

FIELDING A GROUND BALL—A good infielder will field the ball out in front of his body. The top hand will assist in guiding the ball into the glove. Be sure you look the ball into the glove. (Rick Burleson)

and throwing to first, quick hands are a must. An especially challenging play where the shortstop demonstrates the need for smooth hands is on the high-bouncing ball hit over the pitcher's head. Making this play requires fielding and throwing in one quick motion.

Many exceptional defensive shortstops have been permanent fixtures in Major League lineups without showing much output at the plate, notably Mark Belanger, Bud Harrelson, and Tim Foli. Defensively, the shortstop position is so crucial that a light hitter can usually find his way into the lineup.

MAKING THE DOUBLE PLAY

One of the most valuable assets the shortstop can possess is the ability to make the double play. The shortstop has an easier time making the double play than his running mate at second base. He will be moving in the direction in which he will be throwing, and he has a clear view of the oncoming runner.

The majority of shortstops will make the play by stepping over the bag with the left foot and dragging the toes of the right foot over the corner of the bag. On occasion, the shortstop will arrive late at the bag or the throw from the second baseman will arrive early. When this occurs, the shortstop will tag the base with his left foot and throw. This technique requires a very strong throwing arm.

The shortstop should receive the majority of his throws with two hands and at shoulder level. The throw to first base will be sidearm or three-quarter. The throw is

BACKHAND PLAY—The backhand stop is one of the more difficult plays for the shortstop to make and the reason he needs a strong throwing arm. The head must be kept down, and the glove is extended beyond the left foot.

made from this position because it is the position in which the ball is caught and it prevents the runner from coming into the bag standing up. The runner is forced to slide early or to run out of the baseline to avoid being hit by the thrown ball. It will also help the shortstop avoid being knocked down by an oncoming runner.

Another maneuver that will help avoid unnecessary contact after the throw to first base has been made, is to leap into the air, pushing off with the left leg. Should the runner slide forcibly into the shortstop, he will knock him down, but he won't break the leg if it is in the air. If the slide is made into a firmly planted left leg, the potential for a serious injury is present.

On the front end of the double play, the shortstop needs to master three basic throws. Taking the ball near the bag, the throw to second should be an underhand shovel. In order to prevent obstructing the view of the second baseman, the shortstop must be sure to get his glove hand out of the way. On a ball hit right to him, he will "pivot in his tracks" and make a brisk throw to the second baseman.

The third throw is the most difficult of the three and usually does not result in making the double play. This occurs when the ball is hit deep to the shortstop's right. The play requires the shortstop to backhand the ball, plant the right foot, and make a good throw to second base.

It takes constant practice to be able to master the skills of the double play. Not only is it necessary to practice the mechanical aspects of the play, but the shortstop must become accustomed to working with his second baseman.

DOUBLE PLAY FOOTWORK— The shortstop will receive the throw, step over the base with the left foot, drag the right foot over the corner of the base, and throw. (Larvell Blanks)

DOUBLE PLAY FOOTWORK—The shortstop will step in the direction of the throw once he realizes it is accurate. The infielder is receiving a good throw because both hands are held at shoulder level. (Tom Veryzer)

THROWING TO SECOND BASE ON DOUBLE PLAYS—Photos show the basic throw required of the shortstop on the front end of a double play. Throw from where you field the ball. Open your front foot so you do not throw against a locked front hip.

RELAY PLAYS

The shortstop is normally the prime relay man on all extra-base hits down the left field line and into left-center. The mechanics of the relay call for the shortstop to extend both hands to provide a target for his outfielders. After receiving the throw, the shortstop will relay the ball to the base toward which the lead runner is advancing. The responsibility of the second baseman is to direct the shortstop's throw.

The shortstop may also serve as the prime relay man on all sure doubles to right-center and down the right field line. This system will be employed when the second baseman has a weak throwing arm. Generally, in this situation the shortstop serves as the secondary relay man. This is referred to as the "double-cut" defense. The shortstop covers second base until he sees that the batter has at least a stand-up double. He then leaves the base and assumes a position about 20 to 25 feet behind the second baseman, who already has gone out for the relay.

If he receives a bad throw from the outfielder, the second baseman will not attempt to catch the ball; he will let the ball continue to the secondary relay man, in this case, the shortstop. If the outfielder's throw is over the second baseman's head, it should arrive shoulder high to the shortstop. If it's a low throw, the second baseman will not attempt to field the ball but will let it continue on to the shortstop. It should be taken by the shortstop on one hop.

The duties of each of the infielders is reversed when the shortstop is the primary relay man and the second baseman acts as the backup man.

THE MOST DIFFICULT PLAYS

Every shortstop has one particular play that he finds difficult to execute. It's not that the Big Leaguers have problems making the basic plays; they make all the plays. They just make some better than others.

Rick Burleson, the Boston Red Sox's All-Star shortstop, says, "My toughest play is the ball hit slowly to the left of the third baseman. I have to come in, field the ball, and throw across my body to first base."

To the fan in the stands, the most exciting play is the one that requires the shortstop to backhand the ball and throw a runner out at first base. Many years ago, Tom Tresh, a former New York Yankee shortstop, offered a very helpful hint for making this play.

After the shortstop goes deep in the hole and backhands the ball, he should take a little shuffle step with his right foot to get under control. Then he should look at his first baseman before he throws. Looking before throwing allows the player to pick up his target. Taking the quick glance may reduce the speed with which he makes this play, but it will increase the accuracy. It is more to his advantage to have the batter on first base credited with an infield single than to have the batter resting on second with an error charged to the shortstop.

WHO IS COVERING THE BASE?

The shortstop and second baseman should always inform the pitcher as to who will cover second base on a double play ball hit back to the mound. The decision as to who will cover usually depends on the type of hitter at the plate. Normally, with a right-handed hitter the second baseman will cover. With a left-handed batter at the plate the shortstop will assume the responsibility for covering second base.

The exception to the rule is when the batter has a tendency to hit to the opposite field. When a left-handed hitter who habitually hits to left field is at bat, a defensive adjustment is in order.

When the decision is made as to who will cover the base, it should be communicated directly to the pitcher. There should be no doubt in the pitcher's mind as to who is covering the base on any ground ball he fields. Knowing who will be the middleman on the double play will prevent a costly error in a key situation.

RELAY POSITION—(Left) The relay position requires the infielder to face the outfielder, raise his arms, and shout his location. This will help the outfielder locate the relay man. (Eric Soderholm)

RELAY PLAY—(Below) The outfielder has made a poor throw, missing the primary relay man. The secondary relay man will be in proper position to receive the throw and make the play on the advancing runner. Notice how the secondary man opens his body in preparing to receive the throw. (Bob Bailor and Steve Staggs)

7

The Fundamentals of Good Hitting

A young hitter must bear in mind that hitting a baseball, as with any other baseball skill, is based on tried and true fundamentals. However, this does not mean that a hitter should copy someone's batting style. He should study all types of hitters and observe their techniques, but he should use the style that suits him best. Baseball players have different body types and various individual reactions. What works for one player may not prove functional for another.

THE BAT

In selecting a bat, find one that is comfortable to swing. Do not select a bat simply because it bears a favorite player's name. It has to be a bat that feels good in your hands.

GRIP

Grip the bat by placing the bottom hand about an inch or two from the bottom of the handle. Place the top hand in such a position that the lower knuckles will line up with the middle knuckles of the base hand. This position allows for maximum wrist action. Remember, the bat is gripped with the fingers, not with the palms of the hand. Be sure the grip is firm but not too tight; gripping the bat tightly will create muscular tension in the hands, arms, and shoulders. Such muscular tension inhibits the swing and reduces reaction time.

STANCE

The stance selected must allow the player to demonstrate maximum plate coverage; however, it must also allow maximum comfort.

GRIP—Do not restrict your wrist action by holding the bat in the palms of your hands. Lining up the knuckles will allow better bat control and contribute to a fluid, level swing. (Rico Carty)

Comfort is important. If a player is not comfortable at the plate, he will exhibit muscular tension, which will impair his hitting performance.

The stance most often recommended to the young hitter is the parallel stance. The feet are comfortably spread, about shoulder width, with the front foot turned slightly toward the pitcher. The hips and shoulders are kept level, and the weight is evenly distributed on both feet.

Other varieties of stances are the open and closed stances. In general, the open stance is often employed by hitters who desire to pull the ball. The disadvantage of this stance is that it reduces the player's ability to use maximum hip action. It also makes it difficult for the hitter to handle pitches on the outside of the plate.

The closed stance is traditionally employed by the hitter who has a tendency to hit the ball to right, center, or right-center field. It has the advantage of placing the hips in a cocked position so that they can be maximally employed for a powerful swing. The disadvantage of this stance is twofold. First, it forces the hitter to turn his head inward, thereby reducing his visual contact with the pitcher. Second, it makes the hitter vulnerable to the fastball on the inside of the plate.

STRIDE

The stride should be short and low, with the weight distributed to the back foot. Stride to the same spot every time—directly at the pitcher. The length of the stride has been greatly debated, but it is recommended that it be from six to eight inches. The stride should be preceded by what is referred to as an inward turn. This inward turn puts the body in motion, helps to keep the weight back, and generates power for the swing.

SWING

For an effective swing, the batter first must concentrate on keeping his weight on his back foot and his hands back as long as possible. His hands will remain still with his eyes on the ball. This can be accomplished by tucking the chin on the front shoulder. The swing must not pull the head and eyes off the ball.

Acceleration of the bat is dependent upon the hitter's ability to force the back hip to come forward as the bat comes forward. The hitter's "belt buckle" will be pointing in the direction of the hit. As contact is made with the ball, the front leg bends slightly, and he pivots on the ball of the back foot. Some hitters, however, will swing against a stiff front leg.

FOLLOW THROUGH

After impact with the ball, the wrists roll over. The hips, together with the shoulders, must be allowed to continue to pivot with

STANCE AND STRIDE—The batter is demonstrating an open stance and a short, quick stride. (Doug Ault)

KEEPING THE WEIGHT BACK—This ball is pulled hard to right field. Body weight is distributed over the back leg. The hitter is swinging against a stiff front leg. (Jason Thompson)

KEEP YOUR EYES ON THE BALL—(Above)
An excellent study in seeing the ball. The
head stays in as the batter hits a line drive
up the middle for a base hit. (Fred Lynn)

HIP ACTION—(Opposite, top) Power is
generated from two sources, the wrists and
arms and the hips. The hips aid in turning
the shoulders when swinging the bat. The
hips and shoulders come around together.
Allow the back hip to drive the front hip out
of the way. This powerful swing is executed
with complete balance. The weight is
perfectly balanced on the outside of the
stride foot. (Jim Rice)

WRIST ROLL—(Opposite, bottom) The
wrists roll at the conclusion of a powerful
swing. (Carl Yastrzemski)

FOLLOW THROUGH—Study the complete follow through of one of the finest hitters in baseball. The swing is against a bent front leg. (Carl Yastrzemski)

the swing. This movement will allow a natural flow of the bat from its starting position to a position over the rear shoulder. The weight has now been transferred to the outer edge of the front foot.

PSYCHOLOGY OF HITTING

A major part of hitting success is related to the hitter's mental approach to his job. Some prominent Major League hitters feel that successful hitting is 70 percent mental. Regardless of the percentage, it cannot be denied that mental attitude is of major importance.

The two prime psychological factors are confidence and concentration. Confidence is the knowledge that you can step to the plate and hit anything the man on the mound can throw. That feeling of confidence should be present regardless of who is out on the pitching mound.

Concentration is a rare quality that is required at all levels of athletic competition. The ability to direct your thoughts to the task at hand—hitting the baseball—while tuning out all external stimuli is truly a valuable trait.

There are other desirable mental traits. Determination and intelligence cannot be overlooked. It is the determined hitter who looks at an out as only a temporary set back. It's determination when the hitter stares out at the pitcher, challenging him to throw the ball by him.

The intelligent hitter is a constant learner; he continually stores a wealth of information to be used at another time. He makes every trip to the batter's box a learning experience. How did the pitcher pitch before? What pitch did he throw when he was behind in the count? What is his best pitch? Does he do anything to telegraph his next pitch? Constantly alert, he takes advantage of his opponent's least mistake.

THE DESIGNATED HITTER

The use of the designated hitter has become wide-spread in baseball today. At the Major League level, it is employed only by the American League. For colleges, high schools, and youth leagues, it is practiced universally.

There are many pros and cons concerning the use of the D.H. Some say that it allows the use of ten people in a game rather than

ON DECK—For that extra edge in hitting, it is to your advantage to study the pitcher when you are on deck. You may pick up valuable information as to his pitching pattern. Make special note of which pitches he is using to get people out. (Ralph Garr)

nine. Others contend that baseball at the amateur level is a learning experience, and a youngster used as the designated hitter because of limited defensive abilities does not have the opportunity to improve.

One way or the other, the majority of designated hitters in the Major Leagues are not particularly satisfied with their status. Like most players, they would much prefer to be in the lineup on a regular basis. But it also must be recognized that the advent of the D.H. has prolonged the careers of many respected hitters whose defensive skills have diminished.

One of the premier designated hitters of the American League, Rico Carty, offered his thoughts on the D.H. "Being a D.H. takes you mentally out of the game. It is difficult for you to concentrate on how the team is performing when you know your only contribution will be coming to the plate four times during the game. This is more difficult during the cold weather because then you are required to prepare yourself physically as well as mentally.

"It makes matters worse when you are not hitting well; it gives you too much time to sit in the dugout and think. This may lead you to over-concentrate on your hitting. The player in the regular lineup has the opportunity to go into the field and make a substantial contribution with the glove. The D.H. has nothing else to do but think about his unsuccessful efforts to deliver a crucial base hit."

Carty points out that for him to be a production hitter, it is more to his advantage to go to the plate and react than to think about what needs to be done.

COMMON QUESTIONS ABOUT HITTING

Is there anything special the young player can do to learn to hit behind the runner on a hit and run?

The key to hitting behind the runner is learning to slow down bat speed. This may be more difficult than it seems. One helpful hint offered by Joe Morgan suggests gripping the bat tighter with the top hand than

DESIGNATED HITTER—A premier designated hitter in action. Study the level swing of Rico Carty.

with the bottom hand. This will force the batter to hit the ball late, without having to concentrate on it.

There also are other techniques, such as aligning the third knuckles. This prevents the roll of the wrists and makes pulling the ball very difficult.

Other helpful hints are to spread the hands on the handle of the bat, and to keep the right elbow close to the body on the swing. Using either method will force the hands to come around ahead of the bat. The barrel of the bat will be brought to the pitch late, causing the ball to be hit to the right side.

The batter also may try moving his right foot back several inches and striding toward right field. With this technique, use a nor-

mal swing; just aim the ball in the other direction.

I am having problems with hitting. Everything I am hitting is popped-up. How can I cure this problem?

There are many explanations for popping-up. The most common error is dropping the back shoulder. When the batter commits this error, it causes him to uppercut high pitches, and it obstructs his view of inside pitches.

The first change should be made in the swing. On all pitches above the belt, the hitter should swing down on the ball. For some hitters, holding the bat a little higher prior to the swing may help.

Another suggestion is to tuck the chin on

the front shoulder. This technique will assist the hitter in keeping his shoulders level, letting him know if his front shoulder begins to rise as his rear shoulder drops.

Is there any advantage to taking a pitch?

There has been much discussion as to whether or not a pitch should be taken. The great Ted Williams was an ardent advocate of taking his first pitch of the game, feeling that he would be able to gauge how effectively a particular pitcher was throwing. This information could be stored for use in later innings.

Generally, it is sound practice to take a pitch in the eighth or ninth inning with your team behind by two runs or more. Getting on base may be enough to get a rally started.

It is also advisable to take a pitch when the batter ahead of you in the lineup has walked on four straight pitches or has been hit with a pitch. This may signal a weakening pitcher and a situation your team can use to advantage.

The batter may also want to take a pitch when the preceding batter has been retired on one pitch. This will force the pitcher to throw more pitches and prevent him from having an easy inning.

HITTING TO THE OPPOSITE FIELD—This was an outside pitch hit to the opposite field for a base hit. The ball is slapped at, primarily using the upper half of the body. Hip action is restricted. (Ron LeFlore)

SHOULDERS LEVEL—Keeping the chin tucked on the front shoulder and the shoulders level should help reduce an uppercutting problem. (Bernie Carbo)

I have been told that I have a slow bat. How do I improve my bat speed?

To develop bat speed, the young player will find it necessary to develop arm strength. Arm strength and bat speed can best be developed by swinging a weighted bat during the off-season. First, swing the bat just with the front, or power, arm. The power arm of a right-handed batter is the left arm. Swing the weighted bat 50 times a day, using a normal swing.

The use of hand grips and wrist rollers will assist in developing strength in the hands. Be careful not to use any form of weight lifting that involves heavy weights. Various forms of weight training are acceptable as long as they involve light weights and stress repetitions.

What type of adjustment should I make when I have a two-strikes count?

Many types of adjustments are employed by different style hitters. The good hitters tell us that they actually become better hitters with two strikes against them. Then, their concentration becomes more intense, and they have a tendency to battle the pitcher.

Mechanically, the better hitters make certain that with two strikes they make contact with the ball. Move the ball! This can be accomplished by shortening the stride and cutting down on the swing. You may find that choking the bat will help you obtain the desired bat control.

What are the advantages of becoming a switch-hitter?

If you desire to become a switch-hitter, it is advisable to start at a young age. Practice the necessary hitting skills from both sides of the plate. Being able to hit from both sides of the plate provides a definite advantage in hitting the curve ball and the slider.

A right-handed batter hitting against a right-handed pitcher finds breaking pitches breaking away from him. Any good hitter will tell you that a good breaking-ball pitcher can have a negative effect on batting coverage. When you are batting against a right-handed pitcher from the left side, pitches will be easier to handle. They will be breaking toward you rather than away from you.

The majority of switch-hitters start their careers batting from the right side. A natural left-handed hitter may want to think twice about becoming a switch-hitter because the majority of pitchers are right-handed. Nevertheless, if your coach uses a platoon system, as a switch-hitter, you will find yourself playing in most of your team's games.

Another advantage in switch-hitting is that many times during the season you will come to bat with a runner at first base. The first baseman is forced to hold the runner on base. This increases your chances of being able to hit a ground-ball single to right field. This advantage is not accorded the right-handed hitter because it is atypical to see the third baseman holding a runner at third base.

A disadvantage to consider is that you will not hit with equal effectiveness from both sides of the plate year in and year out. This season you may be hitting better from the right side. If you face a right-handed pitcher and you are forced to hit from the left side, you will be hitting from weakness rather than from strength. Of course, it's well to point out that in the long run all good switch-hitters hit as well from one side as the other.

I am hitting the ball well, but the majority of the balls I hit land in foul territory. What am I doing wrong?

Remember that you stride to hit; you probably hit with the stride. A few adjustments might be helpful. First alter your batting stance. The stance should be closed to give you more time on the pitch. Then use a slight inward turn of the front hip as the pitcher prepares to deliver the ball.

How can I learn to hit the curve ball?

The best suggestion for the curve ball is

QUICK HANDS—The batter is exhibiting a quick bat, getting the barrel end out first. (Buddy Bell)

practice. You will hit the breaking pitch if you swing your bat at enough of them! When taking batting practice, make it a meaningful experience by concentrating on the type and location of pitch that is the biggest problem.

There are two prime reasons why hitters have difficulty hitting the curve. First, hitters generally pull away from the curve; second, hitters fail to see the ball hit the bat.

The first problem will solve itself with practice if the hitter concentrates on hitting the pitch to the opposite field. The second problem can be corrected if the batter develops the habit of following the ball into the catcher's glove on pitches at which he does not swing.

What can be done to get out of a batting slump?

There are a number of reasons why a batter goes into a slump. Some reasons are mental, some physical. At times, a good hitting instructor may be able to spot a flaw in your swing and make a suggestion for correction. Let us suggest a batting drill that can be used by young hitters hoping to break out of a slump. This drill should only be used in batting practice.

Assume a normal stance: place the bat on your shoulder. As you see the ball delivered from the pitcher, cock the wrists and give yourself an inward turn. Do not lift the bat from your shoulder until you decide to swing. Swing without taking a stride, and concentrate on hitting the ball up the middle. Remember, this is used only in batting practice. As the hitter feels he is seeing the ball better, keeping his weight back, and hitting the ball up the middle, he should incorporate a short stride and remove the bat from his shoulder.

BATTING TIPS FROM TOP HITTERS

Fred Lynn—"If I am stroking the ball properly, it's because my hands are tucked in tight and I am back on my back foot, waiting for the pitch. I must stay back, particularly if I am to hit breaking pitches."

Johnny Bench—"Perhaps the one big secret to power hitting is the shoulder drive. You must drive your front shoulder toward the pitcher. The moment you fail to drive your shoulder toward the ball, your head will move, and you will lose sight of the ball."

Richie Zisk—"A good hitter must have good knowledge of the strike zone. He must have confidence in himself. I would say 90 percent of hitting is mental, and it helps to be lucky."

Jim Spencer—"In order for a person to be a good hitter he must have a good eye: he must see the ball for as long as he can. Then, he must demonstrate quickness and strength. He's got to be quick with the bat."

Doug Ault—"The three basic elements a batter needs to be a good hitter are a comfortable stance, a bat that feels good, and a good, level swing that allows him to keep his head in."

Joe Morgan—"To be a good hitter, you have to be strong or have a quick bat. Bat speed is more important to the average player, especially to the small man. My bat speed is what gives me the power to hit home runs."

Reggie Jackson—"There are six basic elements in being a successful hitter: attitude, concentration, relaxation, balance, bat selection, and stance."

Rod Carew—"If you're fooled [by an off-speed pitch], you can use the inside-out swing. You start to swing and it's too late to roll your arms. Drop the head of your bat so that your arms are moving in front of it. Then lift your arms and flick, or uppercut, at the ball. If you make contact, you'll hit the ball to the opposite field."

Pete Rose—(Here is Pete's advice for recovering from a slump.) "Pick up a lighter bat or a heavier one. Move up on the plate or move back. If you are swinging too hard, take a heavier bat—it will cut down on your swing. If you aren't swinging hard enough, go to a lighter bat. If you're having trouble with the outside pitch, move closer to the plate; if it's the inside pitch, move away from the plate."

Willie McCovey—(When he was slumping, particularly against left-handed pitchers, Willie made these observations.) "I remembered that I hadn't been waiting on left-handers. I told myself, when I came to the plate, to wait and then drive my left shoulder toward the pitcher."

8
The Lost Art of Bunting

Bunting is referred to as a "lost art" because the skill fails to appeal to the player who would rather be a home run hero than help by moving his teammate into scoring position. This is consistently evident when the big power hitters come to bat in the bottom of the ninth with no one out and the winning run at first base.

Bunting the ball successfully is not a difficult task. Any baseball player who is capable of being on the team is physically talented enough to execute the sacrifice bunt. The ability to bunt is one of those baseball skills at which almost any player, regardless of ability, can become proficient if he has the determination to master the fundamentals. Good bunters make good team players.

For the spectator, the bunt still must rank as one of the more exciting plays in baseball. It may be a bunt employed to move the

winning run into scoring position, a bunt pushed beyond on-rushing infielders, a squeeze bunt to bring home the game-winning run, or a drag bunt to catch an unsuspecting infielder off guard. All bunt plays require movement. The excitement is in the knowledge that after fielding the bunt, the player frequently throws off-balance to an infielder moving to cover an open base. The possibility of error is ever present.

The most exciting bunter in present-day baseball must be the center fielder of the New York Yankees, Mickey Rivers. A left-handed batter with blazing speed, Mickey is always a threat to drop a bunt down the third base line for a base hit. His speed when added to his bunting skill increases his ability to intimidate rival infielders.

Since his speed presents such a threat, the

infielders are forced to play Mickey a step or two toward the middle of the diamond. And the closer the infielders are drawn into the center of the diamond, the greater the chance of Mickey hitting the ball by them for a base hit.

SACRIFICE BUNT

The most important bunting technique a player can master and the one that should be stressed in practice is the sacrifice bunt. The term "sacrifice" implies that the hitter is giving himself up to advance a runner. The bunt should be performed with that idea in mind. Failure occurs when the batter attempts to bunt with the intent not only of advancing a runner but of securing a base hit for himself.

With a man on first, the first baseman will be required to hold the runner. It is then best to bunt the ball to the first base side of the infield.

When runners are occupying first and second base, the third baseman is required to field all bunts coming down the third base line. He is responsible for any bunt not fielded by the pitcher. It is fundamentally sound for the batter to bunt the ball firmly toward the third baseman, forcing him to field the ball, and thereby allowing the runners to advance a base.

There are two methods of teaching the sacrifice bunt. One is referred to as the "square around" method; the other is the "pivot" method.

Using the "square around" method, the batter steps forward and out with his front foot so that his body is facing the pitcher and his hips and feet are parallel to the plate.

The more popular method, the pivot, requires the hitter to turn only the upper half of his body toward the pitcher while keeping his feet planted. Using the pivot method allows the hitter to wait a second longer before he commits himself to bunt. This keeps the defense frozen for an extra second.

Regardless of the method selected, adherence to proper bunting fundamentals is a must. Position yourself well up in the batter's box with both feet in front of home plate. This position will keep your body well out into fair territory and increase the percentages for a successful bunt. The bat should be gripped with the hands about shoulder width apart. The top hand should be about at the trademark, with the bat held between the forefingers and thumb. The grip will be firm at the trademark but loosely held by the hand at the handle. The bat should be held at shoulder level or at the top of the strike zone and well out in front of the body.

Certain bunters may find it more comfortable to slide both hands to the trademark. If this method is selected, both hands should grip the bat firmly.

With knees comfortably bent, no matter what the bunting style, the hitter can adjust easily to a low pitch by bending slightly at the waist. The bat should be allowed to give slightly as the ball meets it. This action will prevent the ball from being bunted too firmly.

SQUEEZE BUNT

The squeeze bunt is utilized in situations where the runner at third base represents either the winning or tying run. When the pitcher's arm action is moving in the direction of home plate, the runner from third base breaks for the plate and the batter pivots to bunt.

The timing of the "square around" or the "pivot" by the batter is crucial to the successful execution of this play. If the bunter commits himself before the pitcher starts his delivery, the pitcher will be able to alter his delivery and foil the squeeze attempt either by throwing a pitch-out or by knocking the batter down.

On the squeeze, it is important for the batter to bunt the ball regardless of where it is pitched and to bunt it anywhere in fair territory. However, the batter must be care-

SQUARE AROUND—The batter will square his feet so that they are facing the pitcher. The bat is held out, away from the body. (Alan Ashby)

PIVOT METHOD—A popular method of bunting is the pivot method. The weight must be kept on the back foot as the batter pivots in his tracks. (Royle Stillman)

HAND POSITION—Slide the top hand up near the trademark. Keep the thumb and fingers well protected. When bunting, the bat should be positioned at the top of the strike zone.

ful not to bunt the ball too hard or the pitcher or an infielder will be able to make a play at the plate.

BUNT FOR A BASE HIT

There are two techniques used when bunting for a base hit. These are the drag bunt and the push bunt. There is some question as to whether a difference between these two techniques truly exists. Consequently, we will discuss these skills in combination, looking first at the left-handed batter.

As the pitcher starts his delivery, the left-handed batter will slide his top hand into the bunting position and step directly toward the second baseman with his back foot. Ideally, the ball should be bunted hard, past the pitcher and toward the second baseman. This is best executed on an

inside pitch. If the pitch is on the outside part of the plate, the batter should lay off the pitch.

Some left-handed batters would rather push the bunt toward the third baseman, especially on outside pitches. The batter will still step forward with his left foot, but instead of stepping toward the second baseman, he will step forward toward the pitcher. The handle of the bat is extended toward the pitcher, and the barrel end of the bat is pulled back toward the plate. It is important that the batter not run toward first base before the ball is bunted.

The right-handed batter may employ any one of four techniques when bunting for a base hit. Each variation suggests a different foot position for successful execution. The batter may step back with the left foot and

PUSH BUNT—The push bunt by the right-handed batter is pushed hard toward the second baseman. Notice how the first step is with the back foot. (Ron LeFlore)

push the barrel end of the bat toward the pitcher. He may drop the back foot as he slides the top hand toward the trademark of the bat. He may step forward with the back foot, getting the bat out in front of the body in preparation for dropping the bunt down the third base line. Or, the right-handed batter may step either forward or backward with the back foot, pushing the bunt down the first base line. Use whichever method affords you the greatest degree of success.

WHY WE FAIL TO BUNT

Failure to bunt successfully can be attributed to both psychological and mechanical reasons. Psychologically, some hitters find it demeaning when asked to bunt. They would much rather swing the bat and advance the runner with a base hit. They view the manager's request to have them bunt as a reflection on their hitting talent. This is especially true when the big hitter is asked to bunt during a batting slump.

When a reluctant bunter is successful in moving runners along, it is psychologically important to reward him with a pat on the back for a job well done. This acknowledgment should come not only from the manager but from fellow teammates as well.

Mechanically, the bunter may fail for a number of reasons. Bat position appears to be the number one villain. Carrying the bat too low in the bunting position is fundamentally unsound. If the pitch is a strike thrown above the level of the bat, the bat must be lifted in the bunt attempt. Raising the bat is the major cause of popping-up on bunt attempts.

Another explanation for the popped-up bunt attempt is jabbing at the ball. Jabbing at a pitched ball requires the batter to lower his bat. As he lowers the bat with a jabbing action, his entire body is going forward and down. This action results in the bat making contact with the lower part of the ball—outcome, pop-up.

Another reason for faulty bunt execution is that the batter tries to get the ball precisely down the base line. When he spends too much time concentrating on perfect placement, results show that more balls are bunted foul than fair. Failure to square around in time also will result in foul balls. When the batter is slow in getting into his bunting position, the pitch usually jams him, causing the ball to be fouled off the handle of the bat.

9

Patrolling the Outfield

Nothing can be further from the truth than the statement, "Anybody can play the outfield." The requirements for the exceptional outfielder are just as demanding as they are for players of other positions.

An outfielder does more than just catch fly balls. He must be able to get a good jump on a hit ball, know the hitters, possess the speed to chase down long fly balls, have an arm capable of throwing out an advancing runner, and know how to back up the play in which he is not directly involved.

STANCE

The basic stance of the outfielder resembles that of the infielder. The knees are slightly bent, and the hands are out in front of the body. The right foot is placed slightly to the rear of the left foot, and both feet are angled, or open. At the time of the pitch, the outfielder will transfer his weight from his heels to the balls of his feet. This will put his body in motion and allow maximum mobility in any direction.

CATCHING AND THROWING

The two prime responsibilities of any outfielder are the basic skills of catching and throwing. Catching involves fly balls, line drives, and ground balls.

For some players, catching a fly ball is easier than for others. Daily practice will serve a useful purpose in solving any problems. The outfielder must learn by actual experience to judge the flight of the ball, to move to his right or cross over to his left, and to turn and make the catch on the ball hit over his head. The "crack" of the bat should tell him the distance the ball has been hit. These skills will become instinctive as he gathers experience and knowledge.

Basically, all outfielders should try to get

to every ball that has been hit. Do not loaf on a fly ball so that you must desperately reach for it at the last minute to make the catch. Attempt at all times to get your body in front of the ball. This is true in playing all outfield positions but especially when playing left or right field. Playing right field with a left-handed hitter at bat, you need to be reminded constantly that anything he pulls will curve away from you toward the right field line. And anything the left-hander hits in the direction of the left fielder will have a tendency to curve away from him, or toward the left field line.

On any fly ball hit with a runner in position to tag and advance, the outfielder should not catch the ball standing with his feet flat on the ground. He should position his body a few strides behind the ball. The ball should be caught at eye level or above—with both hands. The outfielder will then step toward the diamond with the rear foot, "crow hop," and throw.

Remember, *catch the ball with both hands*. It can't be denied that in today's game we have an entire legion of outfielders who specialize in the one-hand catch. It may be acceptable in making a catch with no one on base. However, using two hands with a runner in position to advance is a must. With your throwing hand in position to take the ball from the glove, you will be in a much better position to challenge an advancing runner with a quicker throw.

The line drive straight at the outfielder presents a greater degree of difficulty. The ball may sink, it may curve to the right or left, or it may have a tendency to rise and force the outfielder to make a last minute leap. There are no special rules concerning this play. However, the ball must be played in such a manner as to prevent it from getting by the outfielder and rolling to the fence, allowing the runner to advance additional bases. The outfielder must do everything physically possible to keep the ball in front of him.

On ground balls, the outfielder will be required to demonstrate proficiency in handling three types of plays. The first involves the ball that is hit hard at the outfielder with no runners on base. It is wise to drop to one knee, keeping the ball in front of the body.

If the ball takes a bad bounce, it will hit the fielder in the chest. Taking one off the chest keeps the ball in front of the fielder and in the right position for a quick recovery to prevent the advance of the runner.

With men on base and in position to advance on a hit, the outfielder is required to deliver his throw to the lead base. In making this play, field the ball like an infielder, and throw the ball through the cut-off man to the base to which the runner is advancing.

The most difficult throwing play the outfielder is asked to perform involves a runner attempting to score from second on a ground ball single. Proper execution requires speed and accuracy. The ball should be fielded outside your body as the foot on your glove-hand side touches the ground. After fielding the ball, quickly adjust your body to make an accurate throw. Important: do not take any additional steps prior to making your throw to the plate. The more steps you take, the longer it will take you to get rid of the ball.

A coaching tip: during pre-game practices, take the opportunity to work with the infielders in fielding ground balls. This will increase your ability to field all types of hops.

FLY BALL OVER YOUR HEAD—This is one of the most exciting plays an outfielder can make. The outfielder's first two steps are the most important: the deep drop-step and the hard crossover. Only at the last instant does the outfielder glance over his shoulder to make the catch. (Bruce Bochte)

LINE DRIVE—After making a diving catch on a low line drive, the outfielder should complete the play by performing a forward roll. The roll will reduce the possibility of incurring an injury. (Ron LeFlore)

BLOCKING THE BALL— The outfielder's prime responsibility on all ground balls is to keep the ball in front of him. The outfielder will drop to one knee on a ball hit to him with no runner on base. (Dan Meyer)

CHARGING A GROUND BALL—When a runner is attempting to score on a base hit, the outfielder must charge the ball and come up throwing. This ball is fielded outside the left foot, or on the glove side. (Jim Rice)

All throws made by the outfielders should be overhand and must be received by the infielders or catcher on one hop. Accuracy is the most important quality. Quickness is the second most important requirement. A player will be able to improve his quickness by catching as many balls as possible with two hands and by reducing the number of steps he takes. Remember, the greatest number of throws you are required to make involve distance, so take every opportunity to strengthen your arm.

Following an adequate warm up period, play catch with one of your teammates at a distance of 150 to 200 feet. This will not only strengthen your arm but it also will prepare you to make the necessary throws in a game and provide an opportunity to work on accuracy.

WHERE TO THROW

One of the most costly errors that out-fielders make is throwing to the wrong base. The following guidelines should be used to help outfielders in this respect. Regardless of where base runners are, the following rules should be employed:

> On a ball hit sharply and directly at you, throw out the lead runner.
> On a ball hit so that you are running toward the play, take a look at the lead runner; you will have plenty of time to readjust and throw to second base.
> With a ball hit to your left or right when you are moving away from the infield, throw to second base.
> When the ball is hit for extra bases, throw to the relay man.

Another rule to follow is to throw to the advance base if the runner has just touched a base as you are coming up into throwing position. The following rules may be applied with runners at third and second base:

> With a runner rounding third and just touching the base, if the outfielder is in throwing position, the play should be made at the plate. If the runner is already around third, the throw should go to second or third.
> With a runner rounding second base, the outfielder will have a play at third if the runner is two strides or less beyond second and the fielder is in throwing position.
> A young outfielder should be reminded constantly that instead of always gambling on the lead runner, he would be wiser to throw to the base that will result in a sure out. Otherwise, he should throw to second base to hold the runner to a single so that the double play possibility will be kept in order and the infield can play back.

These guidelines serve as general points of departure for outfielders relative to their basic throwing assignments. Other factors that may alter a basic assignment are the number of outs, the inning, and the score.

COMMUNICATION IS VITAL

One of the most frightening occurrences in the game of baseball is the collision between two outfielders going for a ball hit up the alley or the contact between an outfielder and infielder on a ball that looks as though it will drop between them for a base hit. The inability to communicate can result in injury serious enough to cause a player to lose a significant amount of playing time, or it might prove disabling enough to shorten a very promising career.

We can talk at length about the need for communication and coordinated play, but seldom is a Major League game completed without a near miss or collision. It is more frequent between the outfielders than it is between outfielders and infielders. When the ball is hit up the alley, outfielders find it necessary to run a greater distance at a higher rate of speed. Occasional collisions are unavoidable; anyone playing any position should aggressively go after any hit ball with the idea that he is going to make the catch. The following suggestions are offered for fielding balls hit between the outfielders:

Mechanically, the center fielder should take the inside route on all balls pulled and the outside route on all balls hit in the opposite direction.

The center fielder will take priority on all balls hit between the outfielders. As soon as the other outfielder hears the center fielder call "mine," he will yield the right-of-way. How you handle this play will hinge upon your knowledge of the man playing next to you. With experience and knowledge, you will know at the crack of the bat which balls you will catch and which balls will be caught by your teammate.

On the ball hit between you and an infielder, the following rules prevail:

The oncoming outfielder will take priority. The infielder should not call for this ball; he should simply wave his arms if he feels he can make the play. Once he hears the outfielder call "mine" or "I have it," he will yield to his teammate.

One other form of communication should not be overlooked—the outfielder's "communication" with physical barriers. Any time an outfielder runs toward a fence in fair or foul territory, he should "find" the fence. Once he finds the fence, he will be able to come back and make the catch. If it appears the ball may go over the fence, the outfielder can use his throwing hand to push-off from the fence and get maximum height for his jump.

TROUBLE WITH THE SUN

All young outfielders should purchase a pair of sunglasses and bring them to every game. The proper use of sunglasses takes practice, and it is wise to become familiar with handling them. Some players find sunglasses uncomfortable to wear; this can be overcome with practice.

Some players would rather use a product called Sun Glare, a black shoe polish-like material that is applied under the eyes to deflect the suns rays. Regardless of whether the players use sunglasses or Sun Glare, they will need instruction in the proper techniques for playing a ball in the sun. This is especially important for those infielders and outfielders constantly in the "sun" field.

The glove can be used to shade the sun. If the sun is low, the glove should be held on the sun as the ball is pitched. The outfielder can use the glove to shield the sun if the sun is on the glove side, or he may look through the webbing of the glove, preferably through the spaces between the thumb and index finger.

The throwing hand also may be used to shield the sun if the sun is on that side. If the sun is a factor on extremely high fly balls, you will have time to glance to the ground and back up to pick up the ball. Positioning the body sideways to the ball often will get you out of the direct glare of the sun, and some outfielders will stand sideways to the sun prior to the pitch.

It sometimes is possible for one outfielder to make the catch on a ball that is in another outfielder's sun field. For example, on a ball hit to the right fielder, who is playing the sun field, the center fielder, who is not affected by the sun, might cut across for the catch. In situations of this nature the center fielder should quickly call off the right fielder.

MAKING A DIFFICULT PLAY

Anyone who has played the outfield acknowledges that there is one particular play that causes him more difficulty than others.

Paul Dade, the outstanding, hard-hitting outfielder of the Cleveland Indians, says, "My most difficult play is the ball hit down the line or the ball hit between the outfielders. This is a ball that must be fielded

PLAYING THE FENCE—The outfielder should learn to use his throwing hand to push off from the fence. Using the throwing hand will prevent him from running into the fence and will aid him in getting maximum height in his jump.

PLAYING THE SUN—Major League outfielders prefer playing the ball in the sun to one side or at an angle. Attention should be given to how the glove is used to shade the eyes. (Paul Dade)

quickly and returned to the infield so that the batter is held to a single."

Micky Stanley of the Detroit Tigers says, "The ball hit directly over my head gives me the most problems. I worked on improving myself on this play by playing a very shallow center field during batting practice. Anything hit to center was over my head and provided me with excellent practice on going back for the ball."

Regardless of which play you find the most difficult, get someone to hit you fun-goes so that you can work on your weakness. It is also advisable to assume your defensive outfield position while your teammates are taking their pre-game batting practice. This will help you judge balls as they come off the batter's bat, and you will become accustomed to the background as well. You should ask your coach to hit you fungoes on the ground so that you can judge the speed with which ground balls get to you or between you and other outfielders.

10 Burning up the Basepaths

Baserunning provides some of the most exciting action in the game of baseball. What can be more exhilarating than Joe Morgan advancing from first to third on a base hit. Watching Ron LeFlore attempt to score from first base on a double up the alley will bring you out of your seat. How often the noise and excitement become obvious when Lou Brock or Mickey Rivers is at first base. Everyone in the ballpark knows they will be stealing; it's just a matter of when. As you sit in your seat in anticipation, you sense the constant war of nerves between runner and pitcher.

Baseball fans of every age marvel at the recklessness of Pete Rose's head-first slide. The willingness to take the extra base on a ball bobbled by an outfielder has long been the trademark of baserunners Ralph Garr, Dave Lopes, and Freddie Patek.

There are four key skills exhibited by the best base runners in modern baseball. The first is speed. A good runner will reach first base in 3.9 to 4.1 seconds; the outstanding runner reaches in 3.8 or below. Speed is a must for base running success, but speed alone is not enough for total effectiveness. A player also must know the fundamentals of base running; he must develop the instincts necessary to know when the situation allows taking an extra base. Finally, the player must demonstrate aggressiveness and hustle. The player who fails to show aggressiveness and hustle fails to put pressure on the defense to make defensive plays quickly and accurately.

RUNNING ON THE BASE HIT

There are three basic situations that require running skill after a base hit. The player

RUNNING TO FIRST BASE—When running to first base, use proper form. Keep the head up, arms in close to the body, and hands closed. Do not squeeze the hands; closing the hands tightly produces upper body tension. Always run through first base, lunging for the base reduces running speed and increases the possibility of an ankle injury. (Dan Meyer)

must master getting out of the batter's box and to first base, advancing from first to third, and scoring from second base.

Base running begins at home plate. Regardless of whether the batter is left-handed or right-handed, the first step toward first base will be with the rear foot.

After hitting a single, he will round the bag as hard as he can, putting himself in a position to advance to the next base on a misplayed ball. He should round the bag hard, touching the inside of the bag and continuing about one-third of the way to second base. If the outfielder mishandles your single, you will be in a position to advance quickly. On every single, you should think "double" until the outfielder proves differently.

The same principle applies to the runner advancing from first to third. On all singles, think "third base." Be aggressive; run with reckless abandon. Aggressive running places pressure on opposing outfielders to make a hurried throw. Rushing often results in a poor throw; and a poor throw may mean a run.

On any ball hit in front of you, or to either left field or centerfield, you need not rely on the third base coach. The only time you may find it necessary to utilize the coach at third is on a ball hit behind you to right field. You should pick up the coach just before you round second base. Your first responsibility when you are on first base is to check the depth and position of every outfielder. With this knowledge, you will be able to know at the "crack of the bat" whether or not you will be able to make third base.

Remember, do not get thrown out at third base as the first or third out of the inning.

At second base you are constantly waiting for the opportunity to advance to third base on any ball hit slowly past the pitcher, to the left of the shortstop, to the right side, or tapped slowly to the shortstop or third baseman.

Of great importance is the opportunity to score from second on a single. With two outs and a base hit by the batter, you are off to the races. In most situations head for the plate. It must be emphasized that you should always run out every play at top speed, particularly when advancing to home plate with two outs. If you slow up on your way to the plate, another runner may be tagged out before you touch the plate, and your run will not count.

LEADOFF AT FIRST BASE

The leadoff from first base is a combination walking and shuffling lead. The first step of the leadoff is a walking step, taken when the

ROUNDING FIRST BASE—As you round the base and head toward second, it is important to tuck your left elbow in toward your body. This will assist you in making the turn directly in line with second base. It is unimportant as to which foot touches the base, as long as the inside corner is touched without having to chop your steps.

GETTING BACK TO FIRST BASE—The runner should make a quick move back to first base with his left foot. (Ron LeFlore)

pitcher is getting the sign from the catcher. On the second step, keep both feet close to the ground. An additional half-shuffle can be taken on pitchers who do not possess good moves to first base, on hit and run or steal situations, on bunt situations, or in any offensive situation where an additional lead is needed. The runner usually will be able to get the additional lead when the pitcher is behind in the count to the batter. With the count at 2–0, 3–1, or 3–2, the pitcher will be concentrating more on not

walking the batter or getting farther behind in the count. In addition, the catcher will not be able to call for the pitchout to pick you off or throw you out should you attempt to steal second base.

There are two methods that can be used to get back to first base if the pitcher throws over. The first allows the runner to get back to the base with the foot nearest the bag. The second requires the runner to dive back to first base. Diving back to the base usually means the runner had his maximum lead.

BANDIT ON THE BASEPATHS

Being a bandit on the basepaths will get you the undivided attention of your opponents. Many elements go into making a good base stealer. Maury Wills contends that, "Confidence is 80 percent of the battle. One of the secrets of my success in stealing bases is positive thinking. Like batting, stealing a base is a matter of confidence. When I am in this frame of mind, I not only think, I know I can beat the throws of the pitcher and the catcher."

Ralph Garr, fleet Chicago White Sox outfielder, believes his success in stealing bases lies in his ability to study the pitcher. "Every pitcher does something a little different, but every pitcher will tip you as to when he is going to the plate. Some pitchers, like Tom House and Louis Tiant, are a little hard to steal on because they give you the good move to first base. That type of pitcher forces you to work a little harder."

Every pitcher owns some type of telltale sign that tells you he is going to throw over to first base to keep you close or try to pick you off. Forcing a pitcher to throw to first base is a fundamentally sound principle. Get him to give you his good move as early as possible in a game. If you are the first runner on base in a ball game, it is more acceptable to be picked off by the pitcher's good move in the first inning than it is to be picked off in the ninth inning with the score tied. If you see the pitcher's good move early, then you will know how much liberty you can take later. Study the pitchers for their tip-off signs. Some will tip with the front shoulder by opening it more when they throw to first base. Watch their feet, elbows, arm action, and head for tips as to their intentions.

Willie Mays said he concentrated on the action of the pitcher's head. Ron LeFlore concurs. He says, "This is especially true of left-handed pitchers. I have found that if the left-hander is looking directly at you, he will throw to the plate. If he looks to the plate, he usually will throw to first base."

Dave Lopes, talking about right-handed pitchers, says, "I watch their left foot. If it is stiff, they are coming to first base; if it's bent, they are going to the plate."

BREAKING FOR SECOND BASE

On a steal or a hit and run, the runner at first base breaks for second by using a crossover step. In performing the crossover, the runner will drive his left arm directly toward second, and his body will stay low with a slight forward lean. After the first few strides toward second, the runner will glance quickly toward home plate to determine what happened to the pitch. This will allow him to return quickly to first if the ball is a pop-up or a line drive. It also will allow the runner to avoid being hit by a ball batted in his direction.

WHEN DO I TAG UP?

There are no hard and fast rules about tagging up. It depends on how deep the ball is hit, the throwing strength of the outfielders, the runner's speed, the number of outs, the score, and the inning.

One general rule that applies to tagging at all bases concerns foul balls. On all foul balls, regardless of the base occupied, the runner should be tagging. This same rule applies to line drives. On all line drives the first move should be back to the base occu-

TAGGING AT THIRD BASE—Tag at third base so that you can see the outfielder make the catch. After the catch, push off with your left foot and attempt to score. (Jim Norris)

pied at the time of the pitch. Practicing this maneuver will prevent the runner from being the tail end of a double play.

A runner can tag and advance from any base after the catch. The chance to advance from first on a long fly ball may not be common, but it's good baseball to be ready.

At second base the runner generally tags up with no one out when a fly ball is hit to deep left field, deep left-center, right-center, or right field. When the batter is the second out, the runner usually is encouraged to venture halfway down the basepath on most fly balls. However, on a ball hit deep enough and certain to be caught, the runner might decide to tag and advance. Being at third base will give him an opportunity to score on a wild pitch or a passed ball.

At third base the standard rule is to tag on all fly balls. When tagging up at third, the runner should always place his body in a position to see the outfielder make the catch. The left foot will be on the bag, and the right foot will point toward home. After seeing that the ball is caught, he will attempt to score; it is not necessary to wait for a verbal signal from the third base coach. If he is undecided as to whether or not he should attempt to score on a shallow fly

ball, he should get assistance from the third base coach. Remember, the best time to gamble on a tag-up is when the batter is the second out of the inning.

SLIDING TO BREAK UP THE DOUBLE PLAY

The basic reason for sliding is to prevent a runner from overrunning a base or slowing up to reach a base safely. Never get tagged out going into a base standing up. If there is a doubt, then slide; slide on all close plays.

If a baseball player has been coached to be an aggressive base runner with a competitive, hustling spirit, then learning how to slide properly becomes vitally important. Daring on the basepaths will help a fundamentally sound player exhibit the willingness to slide hard and break up the potential double play.

BENT-LEG SLIDE—Usually one side is your dominant side. Find the side that is best for you and stay with it—always slide on that side. Throw your head back and your arms up as you bend your bottom leg. This prevents jamming your hand into the ground. (Dan Meyer)

POP-UP SLIDE—To do pop-up slides, lift yourself slightly as you slide. Speed alone will bring you up. If you find yourself sliding late, try raising your body into a pop-up slide as you hit the base. This will reduce the possibility of injury. (Dan Meyer)

When attempting to break up a double play, keep in mind that the aim is *not* to injure. The best method is to slide into the infielder with the shin of the lead leg. Attempt to make contact somewhere below the knee and above the ankle.

There isn't a baseball player anywhere who doesn't expect to be taken out of a double play; it's not "bush league," just good baseball. When given the opportunity, the opposing infielders will be doing the same to one of your teammates.

There are many types of slides that can be used. The basic slide is the bent-leg slide. Others are the fall-away, the hook, and the pop-up slide. The majority of present-day players prefer the bent-leg slide. It is best to master the bent-leg slide before attempting any other method. The natural progression from the bent-leg is to the pop-up slide.

With the pop-up, the runner goes into the bag with the right leg extended and the left leg bent under it. As he hits the front of the base with the arch of his sliding foot, his momentum forces him up to the standing position.

11
Keeping Physically Prepared

Regardless of the sport in which an athlete competes, it is most important that he keeps himself in top physical condition. Being physically fit will contribute to the player's longevity and reduce the possibility of incurring a serious injury. If he is injured, the severity of that injury will be minimized, and his rehabilitation period will be greatly reduced.

It is difficult to suggest any one, ideal conditioning program. It is the responsibility of the player to design a program to meet his own physical needs. Each player will have special needs that require an individualized program. For example, the catcher may require special exercises to develop or condition his legs; a batter will use a special exercise to help him improve the power and speed of his swing. A player with thick muscles may need a program designed to stretch and lengthen his muscles, or a player may find a certain part of his body especially prone to injury, which indicates yet another exercise program.

It must be remembered that conditioning does not begin at spring training and terminate with your first regularly scheduled baseball game. Conditioning must be a year-round project if you hope to reap the physical benefits.

Let us suggest a conditioning, or warm up, program that can be used prior to every baseball game.

THE WARM UP

The first requirement for every player is to be sure to take an adequate warm up period. Warming up properly will reduce muscular thickness and increase the elasticity of ligaments and tendons. The first responsibility when you step on the field is to run one or two laps around the field. Next, take 15 to 20 minutes of stretching exercise.

The following two-phase stretching program is suggested. The first, or contraction, phase demands a total effort by the player being stretched. Exercises are done for a slow 10 count against resistance. The second, or relaxation, phase actually stretches the muscles.

The player should concentrate on relaxing the muscle or group of muscles he can feel resisting the stretch. The player being stretched will tolerate the discomfort for as long as possible. When he no longer can tolerate the discomfort, he will request his partner to stop. The partner will slowly cease the stretching movements and main-

Single leg lift

tain the exercise position for 2 more counts. This will prevent any sudden or violent movements that could cause an unnecessary injury.

The Single Leg Lift

The player will lie on his back and raise one leg, placing the calf, just above the ankle, on his partner's shoulder. The partner must be on one or both knees. The player should fold his arms across his chest and push down on his partner's shoulder for a 10-second count. The partner will follow this maneuver by pushing on the player's extended leg for 10 seconds.

This exercise should be performed twice on each leg before you change roles with your partner.

The Butterfly

The player will sit on the ground with his knees bent and out to the sides. He places the soles of his feet together and tries to pull his feet as close to his pelvic area as possible with his hands. The player's partner, standing either in front of or behind him, will place his hands on each of his knees. The player will then bring his knees up and together. Following a 10 count, the partner immediately initiates a slow and steady downward pressure on the knees, forcing them toward the ground.

This exercise is immediately repeated by the player; then he and his partner change places and repeat the exercise twice for the next man.

Butterfly

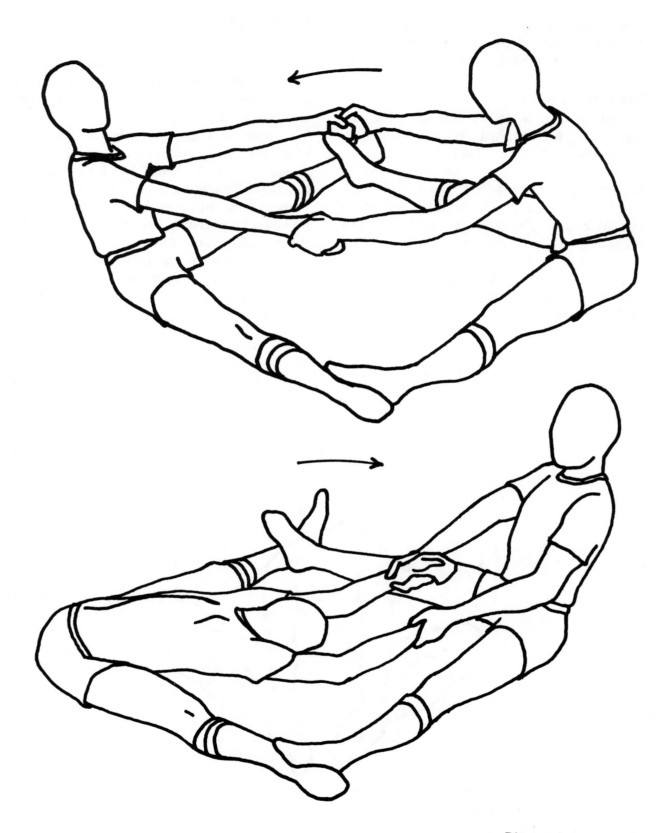

Diamond

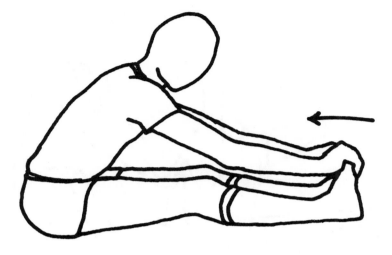

Gastroc

The Diamond

In phase one of this exercise the player tries to pull his partner toward him, using the muscles of his lower back. In the second phase of the exercise the partner does the pulling. Pressure can be increased by using the legs.

The idea is to get the player's stomach on the ground, not his chest or head. This exercise is performed twice by each player.

The Gastroc

The player grasps his own toes and pulls for 10 seconds, gently lifting his heels while keeping his knees flat on the ground. In the contraction phase the player sits and points his toes out hard for 10 seconds.

Lint Picker

From a sitting position, legs as wide apart as possible, the player tries to push back by using the muscles of the lower back. At the conclusion of the 10 count, the player will relax and his partner will push him forward, not downward. The player reaches forward, with his hands out past his feet, as he is pushed. Do not use hands to resist the stretch. When the player indicates that he has had enough, his partner will hold the position for 2 counts and then slowly let the player sit back up. Legs must be kept straight at all times. Do two repetitions of this exercise.

Wraparound

In this exercise the partner's arms will go in front of the player's arms and behind his shoulders, where the partner's palms are placed flat against the player's back.

Your partner will resist your efforts to bring your arms together in front of your face. This resistance will continue for a 10-second count. The arms must be kept straight. The player must emphasize using his shoulder and chest muscles.

During phase two of the exercise, the partner pushes up on the player's shoulder blades with the palms of his hands and holds the player's arms tightly to his body under his armpits.

When the player indicates that he has had enough, the partner will hold for 2 counts and slowly return the player to the starting position. This exercise should be done twice.

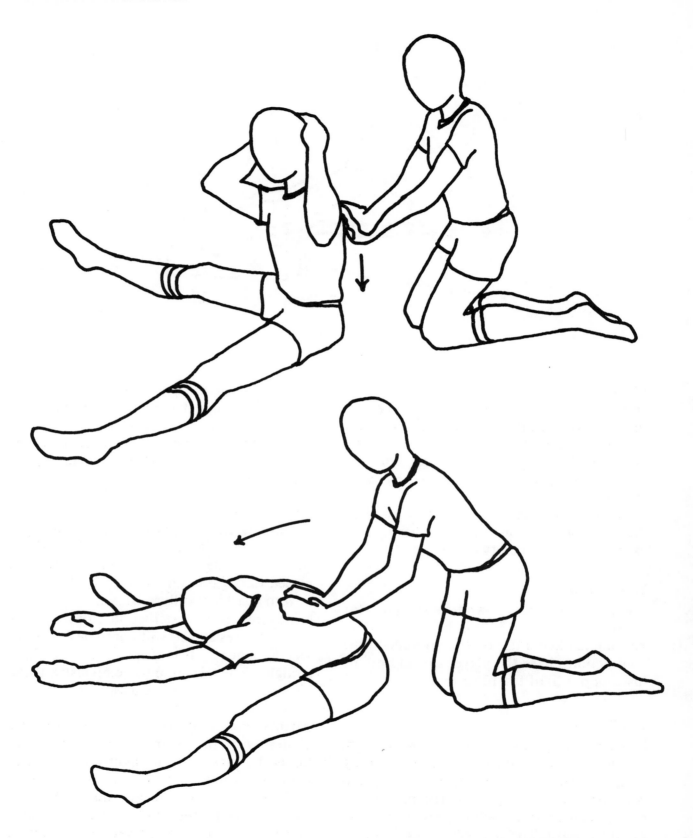

Lint picker

Wraparound

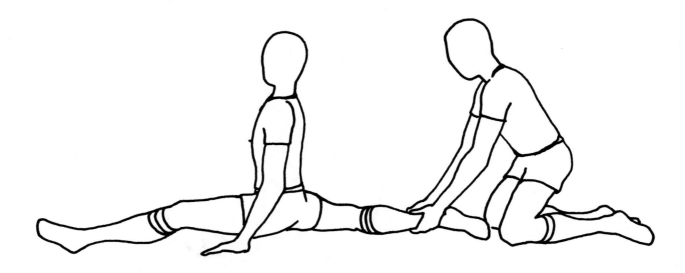

Scissors

Scissors

This is an excellent exercise for first basemen, pitchers, and base runners. It is designed to stretch the quadriceps and hamstrings. During the first phase of the exercise, the player tries to push his crotch toward the ground. This is attempted for a 10 count.

In the second phase the partner will lift the rear foot so that it slides across the ground. The player will retain the split position for as long as he can tolerate it and then recover by rolling over on the buttock of the side extended. This maneuver will prevent injury to a player as he recovers from an awkward position.

Endo

The player will stand with the arms straight back and level with the small of the back. He will be slightly bent forward at the waist, with his legs straight. The player's partner will lift the player's hands up about four inches from his body. For 10 counts, keeping his arms and legs straight, the player will use his total body (shoulders, back, legs) to try to push his arms downward against his partner's resistance.

The partner then will move around to the front of the player and place one hand flat between the player's shoulder blades. With the other hand, he grasps the player's clasped hands and pulls them forward. At the same time, the partner is pushing hard against the player's shoulder blades to keep him from losing his balance and pitching forward.

There is no definite attempt to push the arms downward. This occurs only when the extension of the arms at the shoulders is completed and the natural arc dictates a downward path.

Quads Stretch

In phase one the player will push his leg into the hands of his partner, who is kneeling behind him. The player will continue to push for a 10 count. At the end of the 10 count, the partner will move to a kneeling position alongside the thigh and face the

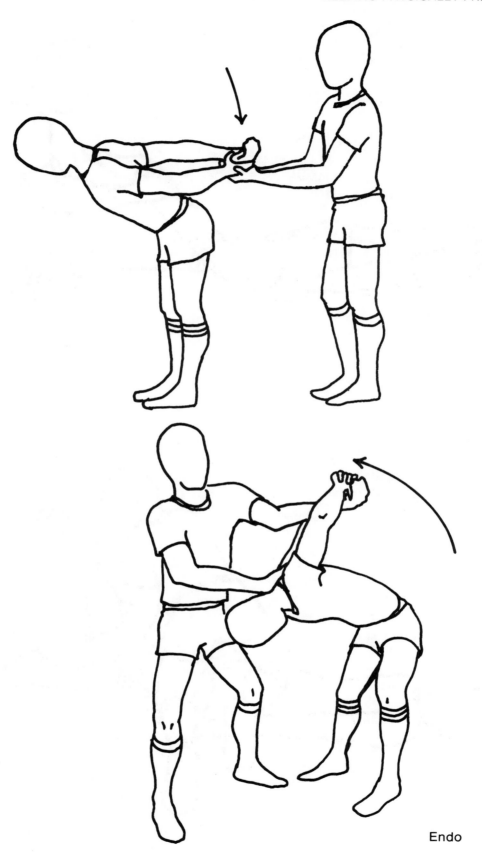

Endo

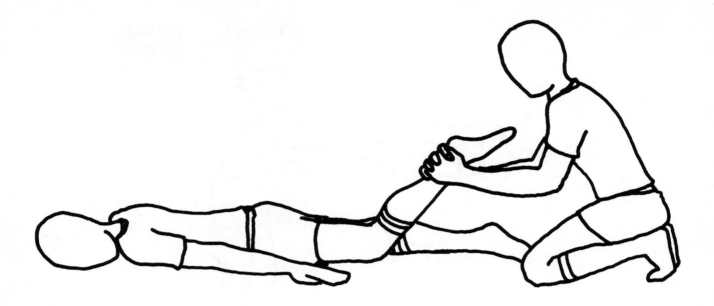

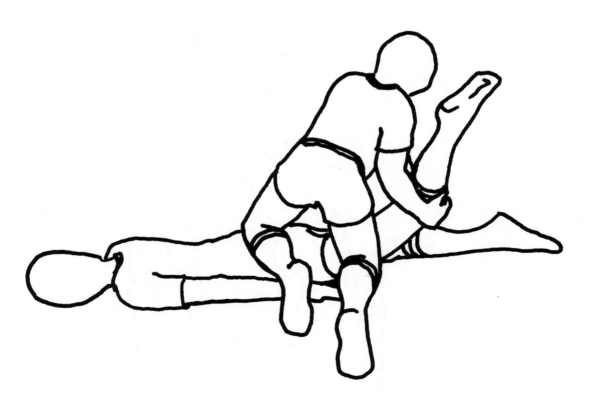

Quads stretch

TEAM STRETCHING—The Cleveland Indians engage in a team approach to their stretching exercises.

player's elevated heel. The partner grasps the knee of the elevated leg with both hands and places his lower leg, the one nearest the player's thigh, over the player's buttock on the side of the elevated leg. The partner then tries to bend the player's hip and thigh around his lower leg. The front of the hip should be off the ground as the attempt is made to bend it around the partner's lower leg. The area to be stretched is the front of the thigh and the groin.

After releasing the leg, repeat the exercise on the same leg and then twice on the other leg before the partners change places.

After the stretching program, players will be ready to start throwing. Start throwing at a distance of about 20 feet. Increase this distance gradually until you are making long throws. Long throwing for an infielder means a distance greater than the throws he normally would be required to make during the game.

Following a thorough loosening of the arm, player's will be ready to play "pepper." Playing pepper is a good conditioner for both hitters and fielders. It gives the hitter the opportunity to work on his place hitting. Hitting the ball to his right is much like executing the hit and run. When a player hits the ball to the man at the end of the line on his left, the mechanics are much the same as those required to pull the ball

PLAYING "PEPPER"—A friendly game of pepper helps keep the players loose.

down the left field line. Not only will the fundamentals of place hitting and bunting be practiced but the batter will realize the necessity of keeping his eye on the ball and meeting it squarely.

The friendly pepper game also will give each player opportunities to field all kinds of hops, going to the left and the right.

AFTER THE WARM UP—A MEANINGFUL BATTING PRACTICE

When the warm up has been completed, the team will be ready for batting practice. Prepare yourself by swinging a weighted bat. This will loosen the muscles used in the batting swing. Take batting practice in two rounds.

On the first round, bunt two and take six swings. You may want to bunt the first ball down the first base line and the second one down the third base line. If you are an excellent bunter and good base runner, you may want to substitute one of the sacrifice bunts with a drag or push bunt.

On the last swing at bat, run the ball out and remain at first base. When the next batter comes to the plate, practice advancing to second on the bunt. At second base be prepared to advance to third on a ground ball to the right side, a base hit, or, after tagging up, a fly ball. At third base practice the walking lead, and attempt to score on a ground ball or break for home on a fly ball after tagging up.

For the second round, dispense with bunting and take six swings. Run the last swing out, and after reaching first base, practice the hit and run. Your teammate batting after you can work on hitting behind the runner. A left-handed batter will attempt to pull the ball and hit into right field. Follow the same procedure at second

DO YOUR RUNNING—Your running should not be neglected. It's a long season, and it's important for you to maintain your endurance.

base that you used during the first round. At third base work on the squeeze bunt. Be sure you and the batter are in accord when you execute the squeeze. Every effort must be made to prevent an injury.

If time permits on the last round, you may want to let the hitter play the base hit game. The rule here is that the batter may stay in the batting cage as long as he is getting base hits. This usually will add spice to the batting practice. Avoid the routine where the batter gets one pitch and must swing regardless of where the pitch is thrown. Too often this leads to broken bats and encourages poor batting habits.

AFTER BATTING PRACTICE

Most of the work on problem situations should take place during the pre-season training period or in the early part of the season. Your ability to handle bunt cover-age, cut-offs, relays, back-up plays, and double steals should all be second nature. However, you need to practice fielding your position before each game. This is especially true when you are playing in an unfamiliar ball park.

Outfielders should take their positions and study the ball as it comes off the bat of a teammate taking batting practice. Make mental notes of how the ground balls react in the outfield grass. If the grass is long, it will slow up ground balls hit to you. This will require you to play a shallow outfield and force you to charge all ground balls. If the grass is cut short and the ground is hard, you will need to play deeper than normally to cut-off balls hit down the line or between outfielders. Finally, you may want to move into the infield and get additional ground ball practice by working with the infielders.

Infielders should work on fielding all types of ground balls. At first they will return the ball to the coach, who is hitting them fungoes. Then they will make some throws to first base and conclude their pre-game program by working on the double play. To finish up, the infielders should take a crisp, snappy round of infield practice.

DON'T FORGET YOUR RUNNING

Running is an important part of all baseball conditioning programs and should not be overlooked. Run 6 to 8 sprints at a distance of 40 to 60 yards each. This should be done 6 times by the substitutes and 3 times by the regulars. Run sprints at one-half to three-quarter speed. Sprints may be run at any time during the practice session. Some players prefer running their sprints after they have jogged their lap and concluded their stretching program. Others chose the period following batting practice. Regardless of when you do your running, be sure it is not neglected. Pitchers generally do more running than the rest of the team. They will run 10 to 15 sprints on days they are not scheduled to pitch. The starting pitcher, on the other hand, should rest in the clubhouse and mentally prepare himself to pitch the game.

12
A Dozen Special Plays

PLAY: "Fill-It-In" Defense

SITUATION: Winning or tying run at second base with two outs, last of the ninth inning. May be used in any inning with a runner at second with two outs or less.

PURPOSE: To prevent the runner on second from scoring on a wild throw by an infielder.

PRIME RESPONSIBILITIES: On a ground ball to either the third baseman or the shortstop.

> *Pitcher:* Will cover home plate.
> *Catcher:* Will back up first base.

On a ground ball to the second baseman . . .

> *Pitcher:* Will move in the direction of first base.
> *Catcher:* Will back up the first baseman.
> *Third baseman:* Will cover home plate.

PLAY: "Bulldog" Bunt Defense or "Pickoff"

SITUATION: Runners on first and second, and the bunt is in order. Usually employed in the late innings.

PURPOSE: To make a play on a bunted ball and retire the runner advancing to third base. If the play cannot be made at third base, it must be made at first base; second base then will be left vacant.

PRIME RESPONSIBILITIES:

> *Shortstop:* Will move in behind the runner at second base to keep him close to the base. He will break to cover third base after the pitcher's second look at second base.
> *Second baseman:* Will move closer to second base and assist the shortstop in holding the runner at second base. The second baseman breaks toward first base and covers first on a bunted ball.
> *First baseman and third baseman:* Play in on the grass to field the bunt.

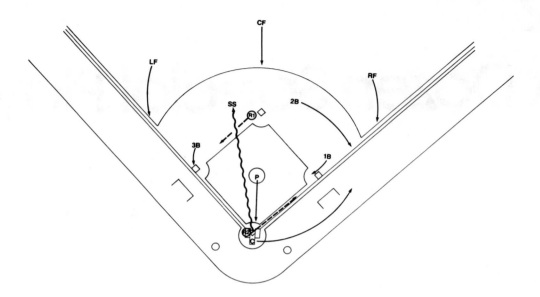

"Fill-it-in" defense (Ground ball, left side)

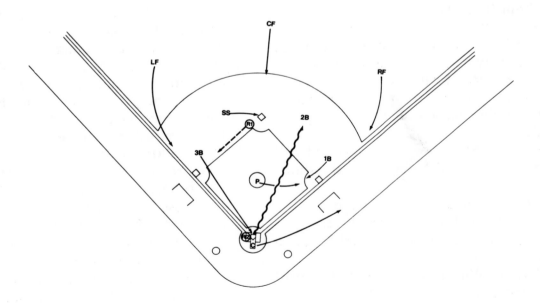

"Fill-it-in" defense (Ground ball, right side)

Pitcher: After taking his stretch, he will check the runner at second base and look at the shortstop. Following the pitcher's second look at the runner at second base, the shortstop will break toward third base. With the movement of the shortstop toward third base, the pitcher delivers a fast ball. The pitch should be one that can be bunted easily.

Catcher: Directs the infield as to who should field the bunt and where to throw the ball. This play is designed to be made on the runner at third base.

Secondary play: On a prearranged signal, the pitcher quickly will turn and throw to second base for a pickoff. To make this play work, the second baseman will play one or two steps away from second base. Playing off the bag encourages the runner to take a larger lead.

PLAY: "Let-It-Drop" Bunt Defense

SITUATION: Bunt situation with runners on first and second. The batter pops up a bunt attempt, which can be caught easily by the pitcher, first baseman, or third baseman.

PURPOSE: To get a double play or to get a force out on a fast runner at second base.

PRIME RESPONSIBILITIES:

Pitcher, first baseman, or third baseman: If a bunt attempt is popped up and can be easily caught, instead of catching the ball it should be allowed to fall to the ground. If the ball is bunted to the pitcher or the first baseman, the third baseman will return to third to cover the base. If the ball is popped up toward the third baseman, the catcher will have the responsibility of covering third base.

Shortstop: The shortstop will cover second base. After receiving the throw at second base, he should tag

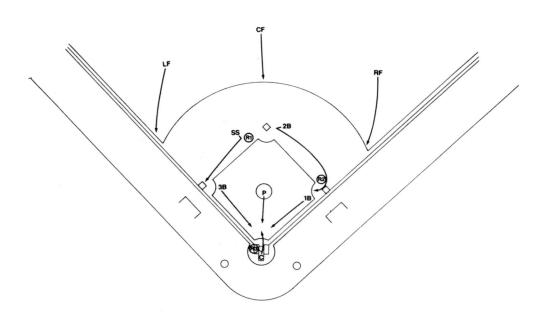

"Bulldog" bunt defense (Runners on 1st and 2nd)
Secondary play: pickoff at 2nd base

the runner for the first out and then step on the base for the second out. The second out is on the runner advancing from first base. This is very important! Should he step on second before tagging the runner at second base, the runner is not obligated to advance to third base. The runner may remain at second base without any liability of being called out. If this does occur, the shortstop should throw quickly to first base in an attempt to get the double play on the batter.

Catcher: The catcher will cover third base should the ball be popped up in the direction of the third baseman.

Second baseman: The second baseman will cover first base as he normally would on bunt situations. This play may also be used with a runner on first base only. However, in this situation it may prove more successful in getting a force out at second base rather than the double play. You may wish to use this play when the runner at first base is fast, presenting a steal threat, and the batter is slow. Forcing a fast runner at second base and putting a slow runner in his place reduces your opponent's offensive possibilities.

PLAY: "Charger" Bunt Defense and/or "Pickoff"

SITUATION: Winning or tying run at first base with no one out. Generally, this play would be used in the eighth or ninth inning in a definite bunting situation.

PURPOSE: To make the play on the runner advancing to second base, should the ball be bunted, or, secondarily, to pick the runner off of first base.

PRIME RESPONSIBILITIES: This play will be called for by the manager. The signal will be sent from him to the catcher and then to the infield. The catcher will require an acknowledgment from the second base-

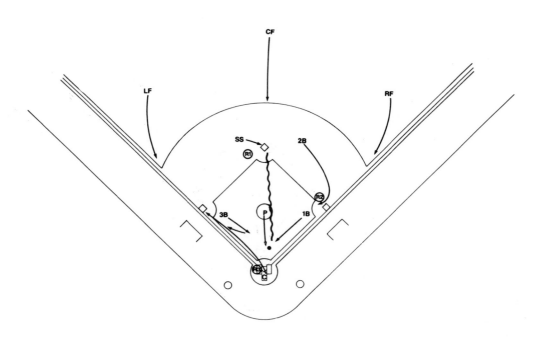

BUNTED BALL

"Let-it-drop" bunt defense (Runners on 1st and 2nd)

man if the bunt defense will be used, and from the first and second baseman if the pickoff will be used.

Second baseman: Will assume a position on the edge of the infield grass. As the pitcher makes the first move of his stretch, the second baseman will charge toward the batter. When the second baseman passes a line between the pitcher and the first baseman, he will direct his pitcher to "pitch."

Pitcher: Will stretch without checking the runner at first base. When directed by the second baseman to deliver the pitch, he will throw a fast ball down the middle of the plate. The pitcher wants the ball to be bunted. After the pitch, the pitcher will prepare to field the bunt.

Third baseman: Will move in on the infield grass and "charge" the batter when the second baseman directs the pitcher to pitch.

Catcher: Calls for the fast ball and directs where the bunted ball is to be thrown. (Note: this play is designed to go to second base.)

First baseman: Holds the runner at first base.

Shortstop: Covers second base.

Secondary play: On a prearranged signal, the pitcher may try to pick the runner off at first base. As the second baseman "charges" by, the pitcher quickly throws to first base instead of delivering the pitch to the plate.

PLAY: "Pickoff" in a Squeeze Bunt Situation

SITUATION: Runners on first, second, and third; runners on second and third; or runner on third only. Squeeze bunt situation.

PURPOSE: To pick off an over active runner at third base.

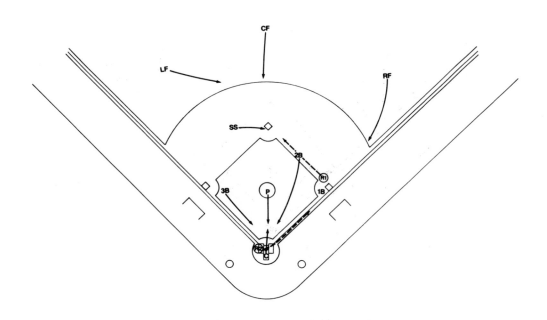

"Charger" bunt defense (Runner on 1st base)
Secondary play: pickoff at 1st base

PRIME RESPONSIBILITIES: All infielders will be required to play in on the edge of the grass.

> *Pitcher:* The pitcher will work from the windup to encourage the runner at third base to take an extended lead.
>
> *Catcher:* Will signal for a pitchout.
>
> *Third baseman:* Must play in on the grass, about six or seven steps in front of the bag. This will allow the runner to feel secure with his leadoff. The third baseman will charge toward the batter as though he is anticipating the bunt.
>
> *Shortstop:* Will break in behind the runner at third base and take the throw from the catcher.

PLAY: "Pickoff" at Third Base

SITUATION: Runners on first and second, a 3–2 count on the batter, and two outs.

PURPOSE: To pick off the runner on second base who is advancing to third base, thinking that the pitcher will deliver the pitch to the plate.

PRIME RESPONSIBILITIES:

> *Pitcher:* As the pitcher lifts his stride foot, instead of stepping in the direction of home plate to deliver the pitch, he will step toward third and throw to the third baseman.
>
> *Third baseman:* Will break to cover third base as the pitcher lifts his stride leg.
>
> *Shortstop:* Will break for third base to chase down an errant throw by the pitcher.
>
> *Second baseman:* Will break for second base.

PLAY: "Pickoff" at Second Base

SITUATION: Bases loaded or runners at second and third. Best employed with two outs.

PURPOSE: To pick off the runner at second base who is taking an excessive leadoff.

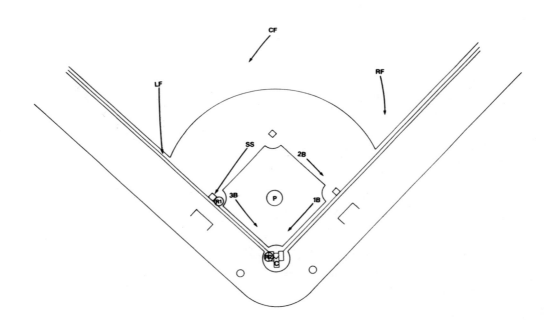

"Pickoff" in squeeze bunt situation

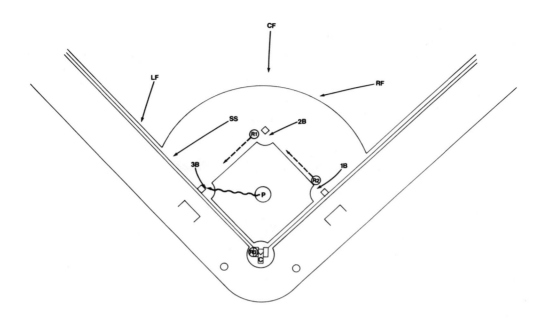

"Pickoff" at third base (Runners on 1st and 2nd)

PRIME RESPONSIBILITIES:

Shortstop: Signals the pitcher that the pickoff play is on. He will then secure an acknowledgment from the pitcher and catcher.

Pitcher: Will assume the windup position, watching the catcher's glove. When the catcher flips his glove down, the pitcher will turn quickly and throw to the shortstop, who is covering second base.

Catcher: Following the acknowledgment of the pickoff play, the catcher will assume his catching stance. He will watch the shortstop. When the shortstop moves in behind the runner at second base, he will drop his glove, signaling the pitcher to turn and throw to second base.

Second baseman: As the pitcher turns and throws to second, the second baseman will break in the direction of center field. He will serve as a backup man on an errant throw.

Center fielder: Moves in to backup second base.

PLAY: "Hidden Ball"

SITUATION: The batter doubles and is required to slide into second base. No other runners are on base. This play can be used with any number of outs.

PURPOSE: To get the unsuspecting runner to wander off of second base so he can be tagged out by the shortstop.

PRIME RESPONSIBILITIES:

Shortstop or second baseman: Depending on where the ball is hit, the throw will be taken by one of the middle infielders. As soon as the umpire calls the runner "safe," the infielder will quickly throw the ball to the first baseman, who will be in the vicinity of first base. The second baseman then will assume his normal fielding position. The shortstop will position himself four to five steps away from second base.

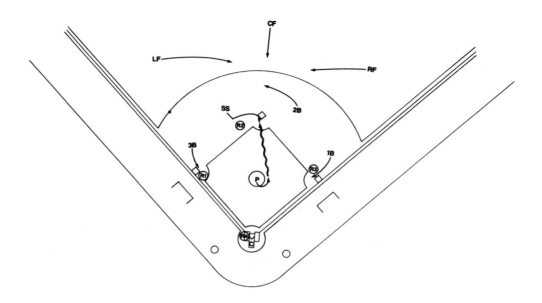

"Pickoff" at second base (bases loaded)

Pitcher: The pitcher will wander off the pitching area and appear to be carrying on a conversation with the third baseman. Remember, the pitcher cannot occupy the rubber or the mound area during a hidden ball play. If he does so, a balk will be called, and the runner will advance one base.

First baseman: Will keep his eye on the runner at second base. As soon as he wanders off the base, the first baseman will make a quick throw to the shortstop, covering second.

Third baseman: Since time-out has not been called, the third baseman must not move too far away from third base to talk to the pitcher. If he is too far from third base, an alert base runner may decide to advance to the open base.

PLAY: "Delayed Steal"
SITUATION: Runners on first and third or first base only.

PURPOSE: To score the runner from third and/or move the runner from first to second base.
PRIME RESPONSIBILITIES:

Runner at first base: The runner will take his normal lead at first. After the delivery of the pitch, the runner will take three or four shuffle steps and break for second base. The delay in stealing second will cause the catcher to draw back his arm a second time and force an inaccurate throw. Secondly, the catcher does not have the opportunity to check third base a second time. The play may be run on the shortstop and second baseman, who are slow in covering the base after the delivery of the pitch.

Runner at third: The runner at third base will break for the plate on the catcher's throw to second base.

PLAY: "Walk-and-Run"
SITUATION: Runner on third base and the

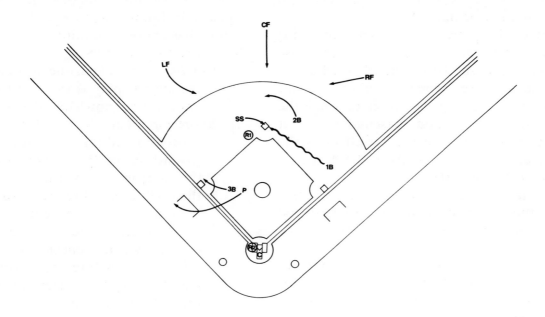

"Hidden ball" play (Runner on 2nd)

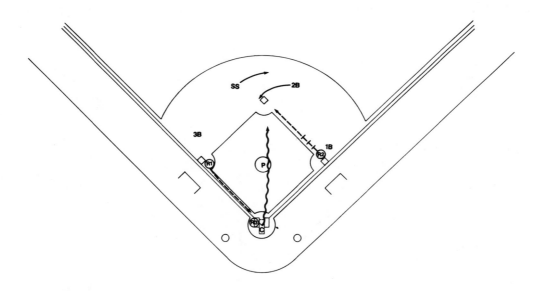

"Delayed steal" (Runners on 1st and 3rd)

batter receives a walk. Can be used with any number of outs.

PURPOSE: To score the runner from third base and to move the runner at first base to second base. This method of the double steal is used when the pitcher is not alert after walking the batter or when the shortstop or second baseman do not cover second base or are late covering the base after a base on balls to the batter.

PRIME RESPONSIBILITIES:

> *Batter:* After getting a base on balls, the batter moves quicky toward first base and then continues toward second base.

> *Runner at third base:* Takes a little extra lead at third base and breaks for the plate when the pitcher throws to second base.

PLAY: "Fake-and-Cut" Double Steal Defense

SITUATION: Runners on first and third with any number of outs. Use with either a right- or left-handed batter.

PURPOSE: To prevent the advance of the runner at third base during the double steal. Especially valuable when you suspect the double steal or if the runner at third base appears anxious.

PRIME RESPONSIBILITIES:

> *Catcher:* Will signal the shortstop that the special play is on, and the shortstop will acknowledge the signal.

> *Shortstop:* On the double steal the shortstop will take two or three steps toward second base. This will create the illusion of covering the bag. He then will break directly toward home plate and receive the catcher's throw on the edge of the infield grass. The catcher will not check the runner at third base before he throws. The inability of the catcher to check at third base may cause the runner to take additional liberties. The shortstop will receive the catcher's throw and either make a play on the runner at the plate or at third base. The runner advancing from first to second is of minor significance.

> *Second baseman:* Will go directly to second base.

> *Center fielder:* Backs up second base.

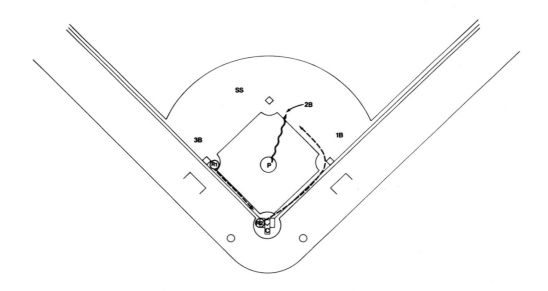

BREAK FOR 2nd AFTER DRAWING A WALK
"Walk-and-run"

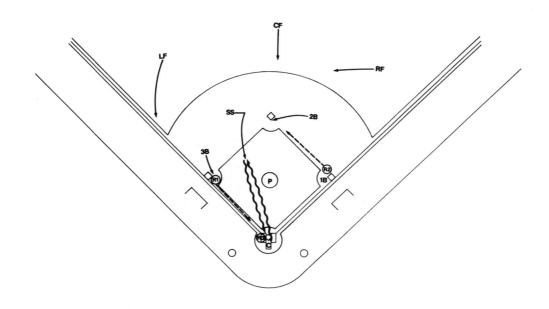

"Fake-and cut" double steal defense
(Runners on 1st and 3rd)

PLAY: "Score on the Double Play"

SITUATION: Runners on first and second, and a double play ball is hit with no outs or with one out. The runner at second base should have good speed.

PURPOSE: To score the runner from second base should the opponents fail to turn the double play. This play works well when the first baseman is required to handle a low throw, questions the umpire's call, or is caught napping.

PRIME RESPONSIBILITIES:

Runner at second base: The runner at second base will touch third base and continue toward home unless instructed differently by the third base coach. The runner must be very careful not to be caught rounding third base on a ball that produces a force out at second base only.

Third base coach: Will inform the runner with a prearranged signal that he should attempt to score from second on a double play ball. If the ball is hit in such a manner that the double play is questionable, the third base coach will station himself near third base and hold the runner accordingly. If, in the opinion of the third base coach, the ball is hit in such a manner as to produce a potential double play, he will position himself up the line in order to direct the runner as he rounds third base.

Runner at first base: Must slide hard into the infielder who is the pivot man at second base. This will break up the double play. The runner from second may be able to score if the pivot man is knocked down with a hard slide. A hard slide also might cause a poor throw to first base.

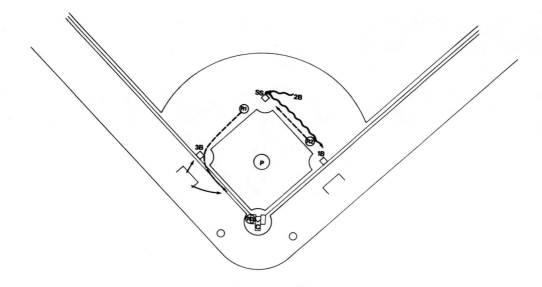

"Score on the double play"

13
Special Drills to Perfect Special Skills

PITCHING

Learning the Spin by "Finger Snapping"

The first step in throwing a successful curve ball is learning how to impart the proper spin to the baseball. A drill that the pitcher can practice at any time is "finger snapping." Have the pitcher hold the ball in front of him below chest level. The ball is gripped properly, with the index and middle fingers on top of the ball and the thumb underneath. From this position the pitcher will attempt to "snap" his fingers. If the fingers are snapped correctly, the spin imparted to the ball will have a downward rotation. The downward spin is the one needed for an effective curve ball. The pitcher must take the time to practice not only getting the proper rotation on the ball but getting the ball to spin at a good rate of speed.

If a pitcher has difficulty learning this drill, he may find it necessary to work on snapping his fingers rapidly without the ball. A pitcher may snap his fingers without employing a downward rotation of the wrist; this is incorrect. Both finger and wrist action are necessary to make this a meaningful drill. Once the finger-wrist maneuver is mastered, the ball may be added.

Pickoff Drill

This drill will assist left-handed pitchers in developing a good move to first base. A good move reduces the lead of the runner. This will give the catcher an opportunity to throw out a runner on an attempted steal. It will also increase the odds of turning the double play, prevent the runner from scoring on a long double, and give your outfielders an opportunity to throw out the

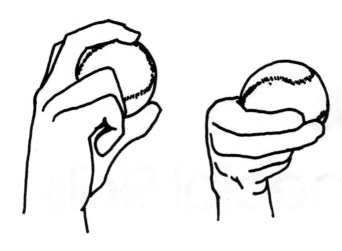

Pitching:
Learning the spin
by "finger snapping"

runner moving from first to third on a base hit.

Place your left-handed pitchers on the mound. You also will need a catcher, a first baseman, a runner at first base, and two "target players." Have the first "target player" stand on the first base line about six feet away from the first baseman; the second "target player" will be located six feet away from "target player" one. Assign a number to each of the players. The first baseman will be number one, the two "target players," two and three, and the catcher will be number four.

Give the pitcher instructions as to what kind of move he should execute. For example, the coach will say, "Look one, step one, and throw one." This command requires the pitcher to look directly at the first baseman, then step and throw to him.

A pattern of verbal instructions may be:

Look	Step	Throw	
1	1	1	
1	2	1	
4	2	1	
1	4	4	
4	3	1	(Keep walking quickly)
4	1	1	

When the pitcher is told to keep walking after throwing to first base, it is to prevent a balk. The umpire will have difficulty determining if the pitcher stepped directly toward home or toward first base.

This drill also will aid base runners in practicing their lead and breaking for second base.

"Heel Roll for Follow Through"

This is a three-part drill designed to help the pitcher who has a problem learning how to follow through properly. It also helps him learn to keep the ball low and away. A third feature of the drill is that it teaches the pitcher to use his body in delivering a pitch. This is accomplished by training the pitcher to roll the heel of his pivot foot and transfer his body weight to his stride foot.

The first part of the drill requires the pitcher to place the ball of his back foot on the end of a chair, with the stride leg pointing in the direction of the person to whom he will be throwing. The person catching the ball will be 15 to 20 feet away. The player on the chair will throw the ball softly to his partner, emphasizing the heel roll of the back foot follow through and the transfer of body weight to the stride foot.

Following five to ten minutes on the chair, the player will move to the floor or to the pitching mound for phase two of the drill.

The pitcher will place his back foot against the pitching rubber. His stride leg will be pointing in the direction of the person to whom he is throwing. The heel of the stride foot will be in line with the arch of the back foot (pivot foot). The pitcher will play catch for five to ten minutes. During this drill he will only roll the heel of his back foot as he throws. The stride foot will remain in constant contact with the ground.

In the final phase of the drill the pitcher will use his full range of motion (full wind-up) and throw a ball against a wall or at a rebound net. The player should be 20 to 25

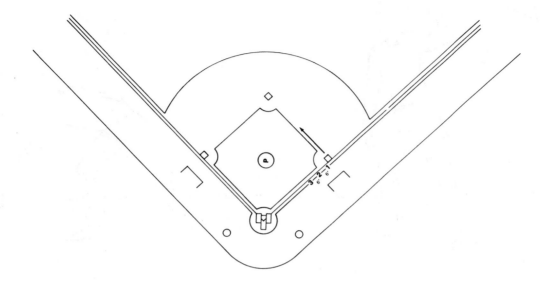

Pitching: Pickoff drill

Heel roll for follow through

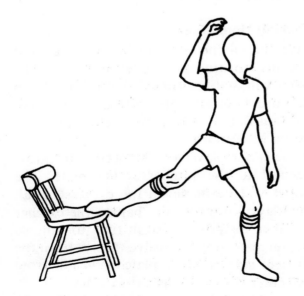

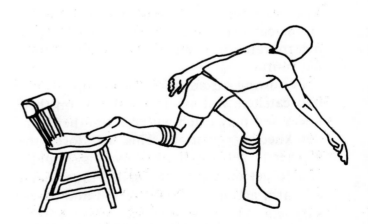

Heel roll for follow through

feet from the wall or rebound net. If the heel is rolling properly, the weight is being transferred to the stride leg, and the pitcher is demonstrating a sound follow through, the ball will rebound from the wall to the pitcher's glove side. The pitcher should be directed to throw all pitches low and away. During this drill it is wise to have him throw slightly outside to overemphasize going low and away.

CATCHING
"Bazooka Drill"

The "bazooka drill" is designed to strengthen the catcher's arm. This drill can easily be incorporated into the catcher's daily throwing routine.

Following an adequate warm up period, two catchers will assume positions on their knees and play catch with one another from the kneeling position. This will force the catcher to get his elbow above his shoulder and to get on top of the ball. Proper hand and arm action can be observed and necessary corrections made. The coach should emphasize a quick release; this is developed

by returning the ball to your partner as quickly as you can.

The catchers should be approximately forty feet apart to start the drill. The distance between the catchers gradually will increase as arm strength improves. It is suggested that the drill run for five to ten minutes per day, especially during the pre-season training period.

Blocking Home Plate

Have the catcher put on his full gear and take his position behind home plate. The coach will station himself 15 to 20 feet up the third base line. He will have a football tackling dummy, which will be used to simulate a base runner.

One other player will be needed to throw the ball to the catcher at the plate. The throws will be made on the coach's signal. The player throwing the ball to the catcher will alter his position from time to time so that the catcher will receive throws from the left-field side of home plate as well as from the center-field and right-field sides.

As the catcher receives the throw, the

Catching: "Bazooka drill"

Catcher: Blocking home plate

Catcher: "Shuffle drill"

coach will slide the tackling dummy toward the plate to simulate a sliding runner. He may forcefully roll or throw the dummy into the catcher to create the sensation of a runner trying to knock the catcher over.

Using this drill, the catcher will learn the mechanics of making the tag play at the plate. He also will experience the sensation of making contact with an oncoming runner.

"Shuffle Drill"

The catcher will be given an ample opportunity to block balls in the dirt. This drill will help the catcher handle his feet quickly so that he can get his body in front of the ball. The fundamentals of blocking balls in the dirt are unimportant unless the catcher can get in front of the ball.

With the catcher in full gear, the coach will signal for the catcher to shuffle once to his right and drop to his knees. He will immediately spring to his feet for the next signal. The coach will move the catcher in both directions, not requiring him to shuffle more than twice in any one direction.

INFIELDERS
Volleyball Drill

This is an excellent drill for infielders who have developed a habit of fielding ground balls with their glove hand only or for those who fail to get their bodies in front of ground balls. This drill also will help "soften" the hands of the infielders and assist in teaching them the fundamentals of fielding ground balls.

The coach will stand 15 to 20 feet away from the infielder and roll a volleyball directly at him, to his left, and to his right. The coach will be able to correct any mechanical errors he observes as the player fields the volleyball.

The player may work on this drill on his own by bouncing the ball off a wall and then fielding it. Note that this drill is performed without the use of a glove.

Pattern Drill

The infield pattern drill is designed to allow infielders to loosen their arms sufficiently prior to taking formal infield practice. It forces infielders to make every long throw

Infielders: Volleyball drill

they will be required to make in a game. It also provides a semblance of order and makes your team look sharp and well organized. The recommended pattern is as follows:

C — 2B — 1B — C — 3B — 1B — SS — C
(First round)

C — SS — 1B — C— 3B — 1B — 2B — C
(Second round)

The catcher will make all of his throws from behind the plate; he should be wearing his chest protector and shin guards for this drill. All infielders will receive their throws at their bases.

Make all throws shoulder high. After making the catch, "crow hop" before making your next throw. Always throw on balance; don't let a bad throw by one of your teammates force you into making a throw with poor body balance.

Two Out Drill

The "two out" infield drill is designed to

remind the infielders that with a runner on second base, bases loaded, or runners on second and third and two outs, they must play a deeper than normal infield position and must prevent the runner at second from scoring on a ground ball.

This means that on any ground ball hit to the infielder's left or right that cannot be fielded cleanly, the infielder should dive to knock the ball down.

In running this drill, the coach will station himself 20 to 30 feet away from the infielder. He will verbally remind the infielder that there is a runner at second base with two outs. The infielder immediately will take two or three steps back, and the coach will roll a ball to either the infielder's left or right. If the infielder cannot get in front of the ball and field it cleanly, he will be required to dive to the ground in an attempt to keep the ball in the infield.

Under no circumstances should a ball get by the infielder with the infielder standing up.

This situation should be practiced as often as possible. Whenever infielders are fielding ground balls, they should take the opportunity to field some of them with this situation in mind.

Four Square Drill

This drill is designed to strengthen the infielder's arm and to teach him to get rid of the ball quickly. This drill also has been referred to as the "four corner drill." Primarily intended for middle infielders, the third baseman and right-handed first baseman will also benefit by their participation.

Four participants are involved at one time. The players will take positions 90 feet away from each other. When using this drill on the baseball field, place the infielders at their bases and the shortstop at home plate.

The drill will begin at home plate. The shortstop will make a throw to the third baseman; from third, the ball will proceed to second, to first, and back to home.

The infielder catching the ball will receive it at shoulder level; the weight will be on his right leg. As the ball is caught (with two hands), the infielder will make a quick throw to the next infielder. The throw must be made without moving the feet. The only movement allowed is to lift the left foot to generate enough body momentum to make the throw.

The first four infielders will perform the drill for one minute and then yield to four new infielders. Each group of infielders should perform five repetitions of the drill.

HITTING

Batting Tee Drill—Basketball or Volleyball

Almost everyone who has played some form of organized baseball has used the batting tee. The tee allows the batter to practice the mechanics of a sound swing and to adjust the batting device so that he can work on pitches that give him difficulty.

This drill is primarily suggested for young players who have not yet mastered the use of their bodies in swinging the bat or have not yet developed adequate arm strength to hit the ball with force. When the young player swings at a ball, he swings with his arms only. The combination of mechanical insufficiency and lack of strength result in poor hitting.

The drill requires a standard batting tee, a "plumber's helper," and either a basketball or a volleyball. The choice of balls depends upon the age and strength of the hitter. For example, if a basketball is selected and a Little League player is working with the tee, the ball will not be hit unless the youngster uses his hips to assist him in generating sufficient bat speed. Also, the basketball, because of its weight, will provide resistance upon contact. The resistance will aid the player in developing arm strength.

"Wham-O"

Two players will face each other about 15 feet apart. One player will have a bag of baseballs and will serve as the feeder. The other player will be the batter. The feeder flips the ball underhand to the batter, who hits the ball into a high fence or backstop.

By moving the ball around, the feeder should be able to provide the batter with an opportunity to hit strikes at different locations in the strike zone and thus afford practice on pitches with which the batter is having problems.

Uppercut Cure

This is an effective drill for helping a hitter who has a tendency to uppercut. Have the hitter kneel down and swing at pitches from this position. The hitter cannot uppercut; if he did, his bat would hit the ground when he swings. From this position, the swing will be down. This drill also will assist the hitter in keeping his head still during the swing.

OUTFIELD
Relay Drill

A relay race is an exciting method of teaching the proper mechanics of executing a long relay from the outfield to home plate.

Infielders: Four square drill

Batting tee drill with basketball or volleyball

Batting: "Wham-O"

Hitting: Uppercut cure

It is a fun drill and builds friendly competition among teammates.

The drill begins by dividing the squad into two groups. Half of the outfielders will be teamed with the shortstop, third baseman, and catcher. The remainder of the outfielders will work with the second baseman, first baseman, and catcher.

All of the outfielders will be stationed in center field. The shortstop and second baseman will assume their normal relay positions on all extra-base hits. The third baseman and first baseman will be stationed in their usual cut-off positions near the pitcher's mound. The catchers will be at home plate.

Two batters will be hitting fungoes; both will hit simultaneously. One will hit the ball to left-center, the other, to right-center. The fungoes should be hit hard enough to reach the fence. With the crack of the bat, both outfielders will chase down their ball and relay it to home plate via the relay man and cut-off man. Speed and accuracy of performance are equally stressed.

Line Drive Over-the-Head

This drill is used to teach the outfielder the proper footwork on the slicing line drive hit over his head.

The player will station himself 10 to 15 feet away from his coach and assume the proper defensive position. On a signal from the coach, the outfielder will break in the direction of the signal. Assuming the coach starts him to his right, the player will shuffle twice to his right, twice to his left, and then turn to his left to catch the ball thrown over his head. Footwork and quickness of feet are important. Outfielders must develop proficiency in moving to their right as well as to their left. After catching the ball, the

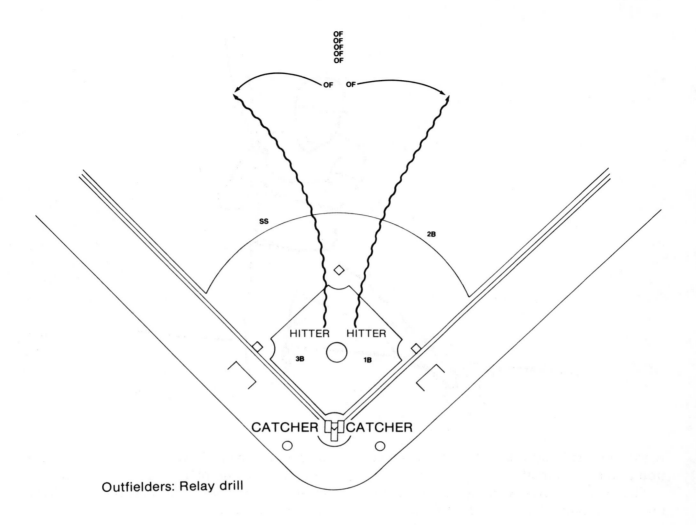

Outfielders: Relay drill

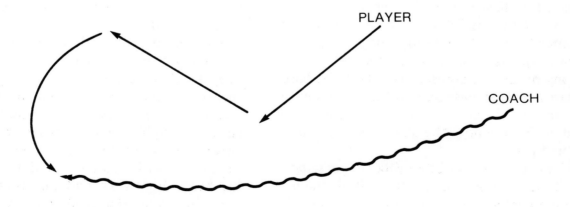

Line drive over-the-head

outfielder will demonstrate the proper footwork required to make an accurate throw back to the infield.

Find It

This drill will help the outfielder work on the ball that is hit in the air; the outfielder loses the ball and must find it again.

He will stand with his back to the infield. The coach will hit the ball in the air and shout, "Find it." The outfielder will be forced to turn quickly, find the ball, and make the catch.

BASE RUNNING
Breaking for Second Base

One of the secrets of getting a successful break toward second base on a steal or a hit and run involves proper running technique. Coaches should train the players, when breaking for second base, to crossover, throw the left arm directly toward second base, and keep the body leaning forward and low.

A method of teaching base runners to stay low on their crossover is to have two players hold a rope about six feet high. As the runner makes his initial break for second base, if he has a tendency to straighten up too quickly, he will hit his hat on the rope. Remember, the height of the rope will vary with the height of the runner.

Sliding Drill

Teaching the basics of sliding can prove to be restrictive. First, the principles should be taught early in the season. Second, the opportunity for practice should be made available. Third, the practice sessions should be structured to eliminate the possibility of injury to the players.

One method of teaching sliding requires the use of either a gymnasium or a tiled floor area. The equipment needed includes a

Base running: Breaking for second base

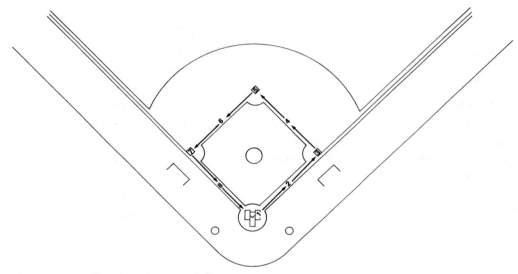

Conditioning: "Catch a teammate"

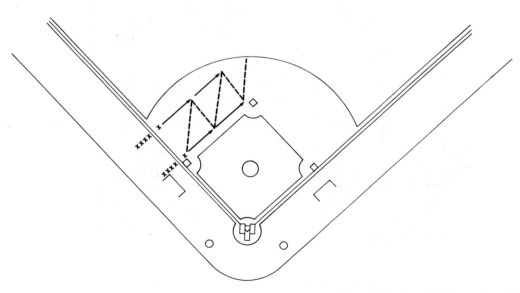

Conditioning: "Flip and go"

base, a can of silicone spray, and a football tackling dummy. The area 12 to 15 feet in front of the base should be sprayed with the silicone spray (available at your local hardware store); this will reduce friction and will allow the player to slide with ease. The coach will position himself near the base, holding the football dummy to simulate the infielder making the double play. The player sliding then can work on breaking up the double play as well as other types of slides. The players should be encouraged to slide in stocking feet, wearing a pair of sweat pants.

On hot summer days with the squad on the field, it is refreshing at the end of the practice session to use a "slip-and-slide" summer water toy manufactured by the Wham-O Corporation. It not only will cool players following a long work out in the hot sun but it will allow them to work on sliding techniques.

CONDITIONING
Power Drill

The power drill is primarily used as a conditioning drill. It involves running, bending, and stretching, and it generates healthy competition among teammates. This drill can be used indoors or outdoors.

Have the players line up six baseball gloves five yards apart. Place a baseball in the pocket of each glove. Upon a signal from the coach, one player will sprint to the first glove, pick up the first ball, and return. He will continue until all of the baseballs have been removed from the gloves and deposited. After all the baseballs have been removed, he will run the drill in reverse and replace the baseballs in the gloves, one at a time.

You will be able to run two or three lines, depending upon the number of players on the team.

"Catch a Teammate"

Eight players can be used in this drill. It is an excellent conditioner, which stresses the proper fundamentals of base running.

Place a player at each base and a player between each base. On the coach's signal, the player will circle the bases as fast as they can. When a player touches the runner ahead of him, he may drop out of the drill. When there are only four runners remaining, the drill is over.

"Flip and Go"

This will serve as both a conditioning drill and a ball-handling drill. The players will line up facing each other and assume the proper fielding position. The ball will be rolled ahead of your teammate; your teammate will field the ball with two hands and roll the ball ahead of his partner. Continue this drill around the infield.

14
The Responsibilities of Being a Manager

A most important man in the operation of any baseball team is the manager. The job is one of difficulty and constant turnover. The man selected to take the responsibility of running a baseball team will share handsomely in its success. However, if the team performs poorly, he will need to assume his share of the blame. Losing teams and player dissatisfaction have resulted in the exit of many fine baseball leaders.

During the 1977 Major League season, we witnessed managerial changes by the Texas Rangers, Cleveland Indians, New York Mets, and Oakland As, and rest assured that prior to the 1978 campaign, the man exchanging lineup cards at your favorite team's opening game may be a new face.

The most important trait a manager can possess is the ability to handle men. He will be saddled with 25 different personalities, each player distinctly different, yet each directed toward the same common goal—WINNING.

In order to lead successfully, the manager must command the respect of his players. The respect he develops revolves around his ability to recognize individual differences and handle his players with confidence and fairness. Each player must be shown that he is an important part of the team and constantly reminded of the contribution he makes to its success.

Undoubtedly, the manager's most important responsibility during the course of a game is watching the pitcher. To know when the pitcher is laboring, when the pitcher should be removed, or when he needs a morale boost and a vote of confidence takes finesse and experience.

The most important attribute a manager

PRE-GAME BATTING PRACTICE—A very active manager, Jeff Torborg prepares to throw a round or two.

INFIELD FUNGOS—Working with his infielders. Torborg spends time hitting them fungos. He can personally correct any problems his players are having with their infield play.

can possess is patience, a virtue of prime importance when working with young players.

His own enthusiasm for the game will carry over to his players and assist in getting a maximum effort from his team. The manager's enthusiasm for the game not only serves as an inspiration to the younger players but it can bring out the best in the most seasoned veteran.

Praise is an effective tool in any business or profession. A manager must take the opportunity to recognize an outstanding performance and let his players know that he appreciates their extra effort and heads-up play.

Much of the success of any manager depends on his psychology of coaching. However, it also should be recognized that the manager has many organizational duties.

Most teams have team meetings prior to the start of a series. If the team is on the road, they meet while the home team is on the field taking batting practice. While at home, they meet during the visiting team's batting practice. During the meeting, the manager will discuss the strengths and weaknesses of the opponents, the opposing pitcher, how to play certain hitters, which players may not be playing to their full physical capacity, and any other subject that might provide the team with a distinct edge.

After checking with the team trainer as to the health status of his team, the manager will make out and post the starting lineup.

Coaches are responsible for certain groups of players during the pre-game activities. On direction of the manager, the coaches will take this opportunity to correct physical and mental mistakes.

During the game, the coaches constantly will remind runners of the number of outs, the type of move the pitcher has, which outfielders have the best throwing arms, and when to tag on a fly ball. The coaches need to check constantly with the dugout to see if the manager has any particular desires dur-

CONFERENCE WITH THE PITCHER—The manager has spotted a flaw in the pitcher's delivery or would like to discuss how to pitch to the next hitter. These situations generally require a conference at the pitching mound.

A TOUGH JOB—A difficult part of being a manager occurs when you are faced with the decision to change pitchers. The wave to the bullpen has become a very unwelcomed sign for many pitchers.

ing the progress of the game. He may want to execute the hit and run or the steal. The signals for these plays are relayed from the dugout by the manager to his third base coach.

In order to minimize any confusion, the manager must employ a simple set of signals so they may be relayed quickly from the dugout. Since opponents have players on the team adept at stealing signals, it may be necessary to change signals several times during the season.

When the opponents are batting, the manager will watch his pitcher work and study his team's defensive alignment. The manager may find it necessary to reposition an infielder or outfielder.

When a pitcher is having difficulty on the mound, the manager may call the bullpen coach to warm up a relief pitcher. Once the relief pitcher is ready, the bullpen coach will signal the manager that a pitching change can be made if desired.

The manager will find it necessary to hold conferences at the mound with his catcher,

"FRIENDLY DISCUSSION"—When the manager and his players see a play differently than the umpire a thorough discussion usually follows.

pitcher, and certain infielders. A conference may be for purposes of making a pitching change, to give his pitcher in the bullpen additional time to warm up, to call the pitcher's attention to a flaw in his delivery, to remind the pitcher how to pitch to a batter in a crucial situation, or to set up a particular defense late in the game.

Of course, no baseball game would be complete without a friendly discussion between the manager and one of the "men in blue." This "discussion" usually revolves around a rule interpretation or a difference of opinion as to whether a player was safe or out on a close play. Only on rare occasions has a manager been on the winning side during one of these "friendly discussions."

There are many duties that provide the manager with pride and satisfaction. However, some tasks prove more difficult than others. One of these occurs prior to the opening of the regular season when the manager, together with his coaches, must decide on who will make the team and who will be sent to the minor leagues.

The selection of the 25-man roster is in-deed a most difficult task. Personalities must be kept out of the selection process; team selection must be made on the basis of which individuals can benefit the team most. With only so much room on the roster, the manager must determine the need and make the selections on that basis. If relief pitching is a priority, then an additional pitcher may be kept; if the team lacks power, then the players who hit best will be selected. It's never an easy task to tell a young player who has worked hard that there simply is not room for him on the roster.

Equally difficult is the decision to criticize and discipline players when necessary. If at all possible, criticism and disciplining should be done in the privacy of the manager's office. This will allow the manager to organize his thoughts and handle the problem without allowing emotions to guide his decisions or comments. A private meeting will allow him and his player to discuss problems that need solutions.

Being a Big League manager is a major task. It takes ability, time, patience, common sense, and hard work.

15

101 Helpful Hints for the Young Baseball Player

1. Remember to hustle at all times; it not only impresses the people watching you play but it may make the difference between winning and losing a game.

2. If you are the starting pitcher, be sure you take 20 minutes to warm up properly and sit down for 5 to 10 minutes prior to going out to pitch.

3. Catchers, always wear your catcher's mask when warming up a pitcher.

4. Learn to dress properly. Nothing can detract more from a baseball player's appearance than a sloppy uniform. Never step on a baseball field until you are fully dressed.

5. Never argue with the umpire.

6. All baseball players at all levels should wear the proper protective equipment; this calls for an athletic supporter with a protective cup.

7. Always wear your protective helmet. It is a rule to wear your helmet in a game situation, but it also should be worn whenever you are batting or running the bases. Preferably, wear one with protective ear flaps.

8. Every ball you hit should be run out at full speed. Never wait to see if a ball is fair or foul; the umpire will supply you with that information.

9. Always offer encouragement to your teammates and congratulate them on their accomplishments. Never criticize or correct a teammate; team discipline is the responsibility of your coach.

10. If you are unsure of any signal given to you by your coach, call time and find

out what you are supposed to do. Don't bluff; if unsure, call timeout.

11. Be on time for all practice games and team meetings. If you are late for any reason, immediately report to your coach and tell him why.

12. If you are pitching and the coach comes out to the mound to remove you, wait until the relief pitcher arrives at the mound before you leave. Never show your displeasure at being taken out of the game.

13. Under no circumstances should you throw your bat or your helmet; such behavior is infantile and not tolerable.

14. If you are an infielder, it is recommended you purchase a baseball glove with short fingers. Outfielders and pitchers should own gloves with long fingers and deep webs.

15. If you are a pitcher, have a pitching toe put on your pivot foot. The toe of your pitching shoe will be protected, and your shoes will last longer.

16. All catchers should be responsible for their own catching gear. It should be neatly folded by the catcher between innings. It also should be packed away by the catcher after the game.

17. Remember, on all running plays that having any chance of being close, slide. Sliding will prevent you from being injured or tagged out.

18. It is recommended that the catcher use a wire-type catching mask as opposed to a bar type. The bar type restricts vision of the low pitch.

19. As a relief pitcher, do not warm up with your jacket on.

20. Always be prepared to advance a base if the pitcher winds up instead of coming to the set position.

21. Never walk off any base until you are sure that you have been called out or the ball has been ruled foul.

22. Remember, on a pop fly into center field, which the shortstop, second baseman, or center fielder is attempting to catch, the pitcher has the responsibility of covering second base.

23. When a catcher is taking infield practice, he should throw to all bases from behind home plate. He also should take infield practice wearing his shin guards.

24. As an infielder, you need to watch for a runner who misses a base when rounding on hits, especially extra-base hits. Remember that appeal plays must be made before the next pitch.

25. Whenever you find it necessary to tag a runner, try to tag with both hands, with the ball held in the throwing hand and in the glove for protection.

26. When making a one-handed tag, be sure the ball is in the web of the glove. Tagging a runner with the ball in the pocket of the glove makes it easier for him to kick the ball loose.

27. Automatically tag up on all foul balls, regardless of the base you are occupying.

28. The third baseman should charge the mound on any ball hit directly back to the pitcher. If the ball is deflected by the pitcher, the third baseman may have an opportunity to make the play.

29. The center fielder has priority on all fly balls hit to the outfield.

30. The best time to get a sign from your third base coach is on your way from the on-deck circle to the batter's box.

31. If the pitch is fouled off on a hit and run play or a steal, the best time to check for your signal from the third base coach is as you return to first base.

32. With a runner on first base and a left-handed pull-hitter batting, the second baseman will be pulled in the hole

between first and second base. Any ball tapped to the third baseman should be thrown to the shortstop covering second base.

33. If the pitcher or the first baseman is racing you to first base and needs to tag you for the out, by all means slide. Slide into first base on all throws from the infielders that are up the line. The first base coach will help you in these situations.

34. As a base runner, never be doubled off on a line drive to an infielder. Your first move on a line drive is always back to the base you are occupying.

35. When playing first base behind a runner, always inform the pitcher. If unsure as to when you should play behind the runner, check with your coach or manager.

36. In selecting a bat; select what you can handle. Stay away from two extremes: the thin-handled bat that will be top heavy and the thick-handled bat that will destroy wrist action.

37. If, as a runner, you are trapped by the catcher off second base, fake hard toward second base and go to third base. Hopefully, the fake will cause the catcher to throw to second base.

38. Never let a pitcher become aware of your intent to take a pitch.

39. Anytime a bunt is anticipated; the third baseman not only plays nearer to the batter but also closer to the line.

40. When a batter has two strikes on him, he should recognize the need to sacrifice power for accuracy. The batter will gain more accuracy by choking up on the bat and standing a little closer to home plate.

41. With a runner on second base and no one out, attempt to hit the ball to the right side with intentions of moving the runner to third base.

42. When there are two outs and a runner on second base, all infielders should play as deep as possible. This will prevent the ground ball from getting through the infield to score the runner from second base. If an infielder can't get to the ball, he should attempt to dive at it and knock it down.

43. On a squeeze play the batter must disguise his intentions to bunt until the last possible moment. If it's a suicide squeeze, the ball *must* be bunted.

44. On a double play ball, the infielder's first priority is the lead runner. Get the head man first; remember, on a double play ball always throw to your partner. Don't throw the ball to an empty base.

45. With runners on first and second and a ground ball hit in such a manner as to allow the defense to secure the force out at second base, the second baseman or the shortstop should be prepared to throw to third base in hopes of getting the runner rounding third.

46. On a throwing play at the plate, the batter on deck has the responsibility of letting the runner know if he should stand up or slide.

47. On a pop fly in foul territory between first base and home plate or third base and home plate, the pitcher should get off the mound, get to the line, and assist in directing the play.

48. With runners on first and third and fewer than two outs, the runner on third should break for the plate on any ground ball that represents a potential double play. If the play is made on the runner at third base, he should get in a run-down, making it possible for the other two runners to move up.

49. The outfielder must not catch a long foul ball with the winning run on third base and no one out.

50. Unless there are two outs and a big

lead, the first baseman and third baseman should play deep and protect the line against extra-base hits.

51. When a catcher goes down to the bullpen, he should take two baseballs, a plate, and another player with a bat. If the ball gets by the catcher, the extra player will retrieve it and the pitcher can continue to warm up. The additional player will be responsible for letting the coach know when the pitcher is ready.

52. On all fly balls between infielders and outfielders, the outfielder has the priority on making the catch.

53. On a cold day outfielders should throw between innings. One player should throw to the outfielder nearest to his bench while the other two outfielders throw to each other.

54. Never leave the bench or dugout unless you have received permission from your coach.

55. If you bobble on a ground ball, never hang your head and quit on the ball. Continue to hustle; you may prevent a runner from taking an additional base.

56. If when tracking a fly ball, the ball looks as if it were "bouncing" as you run to make the catch, it may prove helpful to look away from the ball for a second as you run to a point where the ball will come down. You should be running on the balls of your feet.

57. With a runner on first base and a 3–2 count on the batter, the infielders will field all ground balls and throw to first base. The runner on first will be moving on the pitch. It is also important for the shortstop or second baseman not to cover second as the runner breaks for the base.

58. Work out a system to determine who will cover second base on a steal. Be sure you have a way to convey that information to the pitcher so that if the ball is hit back to him, he will know who is covering.

59. With runners on first and second and a bunt in order, the ball should be bunted hard to the third baseman, forcing him to field it.

60. In a sacrifice situation with a runner on first base, bunt the ball toward the first baseman, forcing him to field the ball. The first baseman must hold the runner at first base, and he will not be able to charge as quickly as he would like.

61. When a ball is bunted to the third baseman with a runner on first base, the responsibility of covering third base lies with the catcher.

62. On any pop fly in foul territory, the third baseman or the first baseman should call off the catcher and take whatever they can reach.

63. As a base runner in a bunt situation, you must not break for the next base until the ball is successfully bunted.

64. Don't slide headfirst into a base that has been blocked; you are just asking for an injury. In fact, try to avoid the headfirst slide at all times, notwithstanding the grandstanding acrobatics of Pete Rose.

65. If a pitcher throws you a pitch that fools you on a count of 3–1, 2–0, or 3–0, do not swing.

66. As a batter, you should help your runners on balls thrown in the dirt. Tell them when they may advance.

67. When on the road with the winning run on third base in the last inning, the outfielders should play short enough to take a good shot at a man trying to score. This also might enable them to handle a line drive that ordinarily would fall for a hit.

68. A pitcher should never deliver a pitch to the plate until the runners on base are immobile. Do not allow the runners to get a walking lead.

69. The pitcher should never pitch if an infielder is out of position. He should either back off the rubber or delay his

pitch until the fielder gets back into position.

70. The first baseman must remember that once he has stepped on first base to retire the batter, the force play is no longer in effect and the runner going into second base must be tagged.

71. On a double play ball hit directly at the second baseman, the runner coming from first base may stop in the basepath forcing the second baseman to decide whether or not he should chase the runner to make the tag. Don't waste time chasing the runner. The second baseman must decide immediately after fielding the ball whether he should tag the runner and throw to first base, throw directly to first base, or throw to second base to start the double play. Remember, the important thing is to prevent the advance of the runner at first.

72. A pitcher must remember that if he grips his pitches too hard, they will tend to be low. Gripping a ball too lightly will result in pitches being high.

73. When a pitcher is in contact with the pitching rubber and a runner breaks for the next base, the pitcher must step off of the rubber before he makes a play on the advancing runner. If the runner is advancing from first to second, the pitcher should step off the rubber and turn toward second base. Using this technique will prevent the pitcher from balking.

74. A pitcher should always do his running at the end of the practice session. That way he does not need to stand around in a damp sweat shirt and run the risk of his arm stiffening up.

75. If a ball gets by the outfielder, he should always throw to the relay man after chasing the ball down. It is not advisable to chase a ball down and then make a play directly on an advancing runner.

76. All pitchers backing up throws at third base or home plate should be at least 35 to 40 feet behind the play they are backing up. If the ball gets by the third baseman or the catcher, it can be saved by the pitcher, thus preventing the runners from advancing an additional base.

77. With a bunt in order and runners on first and second or with a runner on first only, all runners must remember to slide into all bases to which they are advancing. Never go into an advancing base standing up.

78. As a batter, if the hitter before you hits the first pitch for an out, you should, in most cases, take the first pitch.

79. Hitters should look for a fastball on the first pitch, a 2–0, and a 3–1 count.

80. On a relay play the shortstop or second baseman should always keep moving toward the outfielder until the outfielder reaches the ball.

81. When giving directions on where to throw the ball, always refer to the bases by their number—one, two, three, or four. Use this system rather than first base, second base, third base, and home. For example, a play to be made at third base should be directed by saying "three-three-three," rather than "third" or "third base."

82. Never take a leadoff when the pitcher's foot is off the rubber.

83. The first baseman should play even with the bag for a left-handed hitter. With two strikes on the batter, he will back up a few steps. For a strong pull-hitter, he should play deep and near the foul line.

84. The infielder fielding a bunt should listen to the catcher for instructions as to which base to make his throw.

85. The pitcher should catch the return throw from the catcher with the gloved hand; this will protect his pitching hand.

86. All outfielders should take part of their pre-game practice in the infield.

This will allow them an opportunity to practice handling ground balls.

87. During batting practice, outfielders should practice fielding balls hit directly off the batter's bat.

88. With a runner on first base, a left-handed batter should look for a pitch he can pull. With two strikes, the hitter must shorten his stroke and be concerned with making contact.

89. On a squeeze play the runner on third base must not commit himself too early. Break for home plate only when the pitcher's arm starts toward the catcher in the delivery of the pitch.

90. When taking a signal from the third base coach, do not look away from the coach until he has completely finished giving his signals.

91. After a single to the outfield, round first base. If the outfielder bobbles the ball, feel free to advance to second base. The best time to gamble on second base is with two outs.

92. If the pitcher lands on his heel with his stride foot as he delivers his pitch, he will jar his body and disrupt his control. The pitcher can help cure this problem by having the toe of his stride leg point toward the ground as he strides during the delivery of his pitch.

93. When executing a tag play at second base on a throw from right field, decoy the runner. This can be done by standing casually at second base until the last split second before the throw comes in.

94. If the infield is playing back, attempt to score from third base on all ground balls except a hard-hit ball to the third baseman or back at the pitcher.

95. With the bases loaded and runners on second and third, or a runner on third base only, the shortstop and the second baseman must back up the pitcher on all throws from the catcher.

96. Anytime you are a sure out at second or third base, attempt to decoy the infielder by sliding beyond the base and reaching for the back of the bag with your outside hand.

97. The shortstop or the second baseman should always let the pitcher know who is covering second on a ball hit back to him.

98. On all throws to the plate the cut-off man should fake making the cut-off and arm-fake the runner on base. The fake may prevent the runner from taking an additional base on a throw to the plate.

99. The shortstop always should signal the third baseman when the pitcher is throwing a change-up. The second baseman should do the same for the first baseman.

100. Infielders can strengthen their arms by throwing for distance, but this should be done only after a complete warm-up.

101. Infielders should constantly check the condition of the infield. If the grass is short and the ground is hard, the infielder should play deeper. If the grass is wet, ground balls will move much faster and will have a tendency to skip.

Appendix

Losers Are Made—Not Born

A father is many things to his son; but most of all, teacher and idol.

A father, this teacher and idol, seeks ways to mold this smaller image of himself not into his own image but into someone who is his own someone, his own man, unique and self-sufficient and not a smudged carbon copy of someone else.

And one of the ways this teacher and idol knows and also explores to help his son reach manhood and maturity simultaneously is sports.

For sports reveal to his son that life is a struggle, that skills to handle this struggle must be studied and learned and meshed with the skills of others so that which must be accomplished is accomplished.

Sports also show his son that every struggle has an uncertain outcome no matter what skills he commands. For in every contest chance plays the starring role or calls signals from the bench.

Sport show his son in telescoped time what his father most wants him to know.

The game is never over no matter what the scoreboard reads, no matter what the clock says. The secret of the game is to do one's best, to persist and endure, and, as someone said, to strive, to seek, to find, and not to yield.

A Team Prayer

Almighty God, You who are called the Great Umpire, in this game of life we are unsure as to what uniform we should wear.

While we may be Angels in spirit, in reality we are Giants in pride, Dodgers of responsibility, and Tigers in ambition.

When it comes to faith, we find ourselves in the minor leagues.

When it comes to good works, we strike out.

When it comes to knowledge of Your word, we are not even sure of the ground rules.

Therefore, we're thankful for Your mercy when we are in foul territory, for Your forgiveness when we commit one error after another, for Your uplifting spirit when we are in the pitfalls of a slump.

Oh, God, let our game-plan be Your will and our response a sellout crowd with standing room only.

And when our number is retired here on earth, may we head for Your home base and rejoice to hear You call out, "Safe."

In the name of Him who gives the final victory to all who believe, Christ our Lord,

Amen.

Scoreboard for a Winner
(how to tell a winner from a loser)

A winner says, "Let's find out"; a loser says, "Nobody knows."

When a winner makes a mistake, he says, "I was wrong"; when a loser makes a mistake, he says, "It wasn't my fault."

A winner credits his "good luck" for winning—even though it isn't good luck; a loser blames his "bad luck" for losing—even though it isn't bad luck.

A winner knows how and when to say "yes" and "no"; a loser says, "Yes, but . . . " and, "Perhaps not" at the wrong times for the wrong reasons.

A winner isn't nearly as afraid of losing as a loser is secretly afraid of winning. *A winner works harder than a loser* and has more time; a loser is always "too busy" to do what is necessary.

A winner goes *through* a problem; a loser goes *around* it and never gets past it.

A winner makes commitments; a loser makes promises. A winner shows he's sorry by making up for it; a loser says, "I'm sorry," but does the same thing next time.

A winner knows what to fight for and what to compromise on; a loser compromises on what he shouldn't and fights for what isn't worth fighting for.

A winner says, "I'm good, *but not as good as I should be."* A loser says, "I'm not as bad as a lot of other people."

A winner *listens;* a loser just waits until it's his turn to talk. A winner would rather be admired than liked, although he would prefer both; a loser would rather be liked than admired, and is even willing to pay the price of mild contempt for it.

A winner feels strongly enough to be gentle; a loser is never gentle—he is either weak or pettily tyrannous by turns.

A winner *respects those who are superior to him and tries to learn* something from them; a loser resents those who are superior to him and tries to find chinks in their armor.

A winner explains; a loser explains away. A winner feels responsible for more than his job; a loser says, "I only work here." A winner says, "There ought to be a better way to do it"; a loser says, "That's the way it's always been done here."

A winner paces himself; a loser has only two speeds: Hysterical and Lethargic!

The Game Guy's Prayer

Dear God:

Help me to be a sport in this little Game of Life. I don't ask for any place in the lineup; play me where You need me. I only ask for the stuff to give You one hundred percent of what I've got. If all the hard drives come my way, I thank You for the compliment. Help me to remember that You won't let anything come that You and I together can't handle. And help me to take the bad breaks as part of the Game. Help me to be thankful for them.

And, God, help me always to play on the square, no matter what the other players do. Help me to come clean. Help me to see that often the best part of the Game is helping other guys. Help me to be a regular fellow with the other players.

Finally, God, if fate seems to uppercut me with both hands and I'm laid up on the shelf in sickness or pain, help me to take that as a part of the Game, too.

Help me not to whimper or squeal that the Game was a frame-up or that I had a raw deal. When in the dusk I get the final bell, I ask for no lying, complimentary stones—I only want to know that You feel I've been a good guy.

How Best Not to Get Along with Coach and Teammates

Be late to practice often.

Never hustle.

Pass a signal—this confuses the opposition.

When bunting, use a pool cue; get on your toes and run before you bunt.

Don't run batted balls out (opposition never makes an error)—sure out, anyway.

Don't touch the bases. We are trying to save money and the bases.

Loaf going to all bases on batted balls; save your legs for the bench—tired blood.

Don't do any thinking of your own when running bases; you can always blame the coaches.

Take a big chance between second and third bases, especially with none out—kills rally.

Get doubled off third base on a line drive—this shows you are alert and eager.

Swing a long, heavy bat as hard as you can—be a man.

Make a practice of throwing behind the runner—this keeps a rally going for opponents.

Get caught off base in scoring position (especially third base).

Don't slide—it saves the uniform and eliminates the strawberries.

See how far you can throw your bat after striking out.

Throw your glove down, step on it with your spikes—glove should not have dropped the ball.

Never read a rule book—you know too much now.

Always disagree with umpire—this is a sure way to get in the social register.

Never run in and out between innings—this makes the game go too fast.

Great Players

Great athletes come in all sizes, but they have some common characteristics:

Great players are STRONG

Great players have STAMINA.

Great players are CAT-LIKE.

Great players MAKE the KEY PLAYS in the situations that count.

Great players are DEDICATED and have a burning desire to win. They don't take a loss lightly.

Success

Success in Baseball, like *success* in any sport or profession, is a frame of mind. More players fail mentally than physically. The young man who acquires a proper mental attitude toward the game and along with it realizes that most *Successful Baseball Players* are *made,* not *born,* will be on the road to *Success* and should have no difficulty in becoming reasonably adept at this great game.

The road to development of one's best self is not easy. But it is especially difficult for the young man who thinks *Success* can be attained by some "hocus-pocus" or

"Ouija board" method. If a player is willing to work both physically and mentally and will give the various suggestions that follow an honest try, he will develop his talents to a high degree and have the time of his life doing it.

He must resolve to be honest with himself and pursue his course to the very end if he hopes to acquire mental attitudes that will prove beneficial both in *Baseball* and life. The payoff in athletics goes to the one who aspires to be outstanding and does not overlook any detail that contributes to *Success.* He pays special attention to weaknesses, keeps an open mind, and tests especially those ideas he is inclined to doubt. Failure is the lot of the athlete who thinks he knows all the answers, while *Success* comes to the athlete who is inclined to listen to wise counsel.   Compliments of:
Tom Noland, Baseball Coach,
Lincoln Park High School

A Baseball Prayer

It's important to me Lord. To some, it's only a game that will be forgotten when they leave the park.

To those of us who have sacrificed countless hours of the precious time You have granted us on Your earth it becomes more important.

We don't expect you to swing the bat or handle the glove for us, Lord,

But we do ask that You make us aware of the ability that You have bestowed upon us.

Please don't let us allow this gift to pass on, unnoticed.

We ask
that when the time comes
when we no longer have fun
displaying the skills that You have blessed
so few of us with,
that we will àt least
have the courtesy and courage
to put our suit away.

Lord, we thank you for the courage, the strength, the ability, and speed to perform

for those that are appreciative of this rare ability that You have bestowed upon us.

In Your name we ask this,

Amen.

by PAT DAUGHERTY

Clutch Player Qualities*

He aspires to develop those traits that make him best when competition is toughest so that he will let nothing stand in the way of attaining them.

He has a team spirit and prefers team victory to personal glory.

He likes to see the other fellow succeed.

He keeps in good physical condition at all times.

He deals honestly with coach and teammates.

He never blames anyone for his failures, accepting the responsibility himself.

He strives to master all details of the game.

He understands percentages and knows that one failure does not mean a succession of failures but is only percentage at work.

He is gracious in defeat; for this reason he is not tense in a tight spot. The player who sees defeat and victory in proper proportion is cool under fire. This is one secret of relaxation.

He realizes that differences between most players are not so great that intelligent work cannot overcome them.

He has a friendly, competitive attitude toward his opponents.

He loves to play for the pleasure of playing and strives to overcome weaknesses.

He has a well-balanced outlook on life with sufficient other interests to keep a single one from becoming a stumbling block to success if he fails at it.

He studies the qualities of clutch players, past and present.

---

*Note: Clutch players are scarce only because most athletes refuse to believe the clutch player possesses a combination of qualities that he could have if he were willing to work for them.

He cultivates kindliness, friendliness, and unselfishness.

He cultivates a charitable spirit; hence, he is not puffed up.

He knows the sun will rise again in the morning whether he hits a home run or strikes out.

Finally, he realizes that he will forget "self" when he cultivates the qualities above. He is oblivious of "self"; hence, he can perform in the clutch because he does not experience the tenseness and over-anxiety that always mark the self-centered person.

The Indispensable Man

Sometime, when you're feeling important,
  Sometime, when your ego's in bloom,
Sometime, when you take it for granted
  You're the best qualified in the room.
Sometime, when you feel that your going
  Would leave an unfillable hole,
Just follow this simple instruction
  And see how it humbles your soul.
Take a bucket and fill it with water:
  Put your hand in it up to the wrist;
Pull it out, and the hole that's remaining
  Is a measure of how you'll be missed.
You may splash all you please when you enter,
  You can stir up the water galore,
But stop, and you'll find in a minute
  That it looks quite the same as before.
The moral in this quaint example
  Is to do just the best that you can.
Be proud of yourself, but remember,
  There's no indispensable man!

Drills, Drills, Drills!

The baseball coach was mighty tough,
  He never seemed to get enough
Of drills and drills and drills and drills,
  Until it seemed he wished to kill.
The players made a lot of fuss
  And said, "He's making fools of us!
Now, what's the use of all that stuff,
  We know those plays all well enough.
If he would let us play a game,

We'd use all those plays just the same."
At last there came the longed-for day
  When they had THE big game to play.
And then those weeks of constant drill
  Began to show in baseball skill.
The team would make their double plays
  And shine in lots of other ways.
They'd catch a runner off at first,
  The way they often had rehearsed.
And if one tried a hit to stretch,
  They always got the sorry wretch.
And when they came to bat themselves,
  They acted like uprightly elves.
They made their double steals with ease,
  And did just about as they'd please.
They bunted in a man from third
  And made the pitcher look absurd.
And when the game was played and won,
  They said, "Oh, boy, but that was fun.
Hey Coach, we want to drill some more,
  And next time make a bigger score!"

Written and Contributed by
Raymond F. Bellamy

The Ten Commandments of Baseball

Nobody ever became a ballplayer by walking after a ball.

You will never become a .300 hitter unless you take the bat off your shoulder.

Outfielders who throw the ball back of the runner lock the barn after the horse is stolen.

Keep your head up and you may not have to hold it down.

When you start to slide—slide! He who changes his mind changes a good leg for a broken one.

Don't quit. The game is never over until the last man is out.

Always run them out. You never can tell.

Don't alibi on the bad hops. Anybody can field the good ones.

Don't find too many faults with the umpires. You can't expect them to be as perfect as you are.

A pitcher who hasn't control, hasn't anything.

The Whole Ball Player

CAN BE SEEN WITH EYE

INFIELDER-OUTFIELDER

PITCHER

ARM STRENGTH
USE OF ARM
SPEED
HANDS
FIELDING
RANGE
HITTING
POWER

ARM STRENGTH
FAST BALL
CURVE BALL
OFF-PITCH
CONTROL

CATCHER

ARM STRENGTH
USE OF ARM
HANDS
RECEIVING
HITTING
POWER
SPEED

GENERAL FOR ALL PLAYERS

STAMINA
DURABILITY
ANTICIPATION

RECORD IF IN PRO BALL

REFLEXES   COORDINATION
SIZE   AGILITY

POISE
INSTINCT
BASE RUNNING

ATTITUDE

DESIRE
DRIVE
WILLINGNESS
HUNGER
AMBITION

MENTAL

INTELLIGENCE
BASEBALL SENSE
TEACHABILITY
KNOWLEDGE OF GAME

WINNER

STOMACH
HEART
COMPETITOR
PRIDE
CONFIDENCE

PERSONALITY

IMPROVEMENT
CONSISTENCY
MATURITY
ADJUSTMENT
STABILITY
TEMPERAMENT
DISPOSITION

BACKGROUND

FAMILY
HABITS

CANNOT BE SEEN WITH EYE

If you do not feel you have sufficient knowledge to judge a player in a particular category, please circle it.

CODE: Player must be classified as good (3) or excellent (4) in each of the above categories or the word in the circle should be crossed out.

Index